# BUSINESS BLOCKS

## TRANSFORM YOUR SELF-SABOTAGING MIND GREMLINS, AWAKEN YOUR INNER MENTOR, AND ALLOW YOUR BUSINESS BRILLIANCE TO SHINE

HOLLY WORTON

A CIP catalogue record for this book is available from the British Library



First edition: 2016
Second edition: 2020

Published by Tribal Publishing Ltd

Please direct permissions requests to:
permissions@tribal-publishing.com

# CONTENTS

# INTRODUCTION TO THE SECOND EDITION

This book, *Business Blocks*, was my second business mindset book (following *Business Beliefs*). Since then, I have released two others, both of which (*Business Visibility* and *Business Intuition*) are complementary to the first two. I've received great feedback from all the books, and I'm currently planning to release second editions of them all in 2020.

It's been almost four years since I launched the first edition of this book, and I'm very excited to be releasing this expanded second edition. My main goal is to make this content even more useful to people: the first edition was available only as an ebook. I initially decided to release these books in electronic format in part because the book was concise. I intended to provide only the most basic information that people would need to get started identifying and transforming their business blocks. I didn't want readers to get caught up in theory; I wanted them to get the knowledge they needed to start taking action. I wanted it to be a practical, useful book, and not what a former coach of mine used to call "shelf help" books, which are mildly inspirational for a short period until they go back on your bookshelf like every other book.

But I realized that these four business mindset titles would be much more useful as paperbacks. I prefer to read nonfiction books in print because it makes it easier for me to underline them, make notes in the margins, and keep them on hand for reference. And while I don't particularly enjoy audiobooks—I find it difficult to absorb and retain the material by ear—I know that there are plenty of people who don't read print or ebooks at all, preferring audiobooks for their reading. That's why I'm making this second edition available as an ebook, paperback, and audiobook.

Perhaps the most exciting part of producing this second edition is that I'm also releasing a companion workbook to go along with this book. Creating a workbook for this title is something I've wanted to do for ages, and after I published the companion workbook for my 2019 title *If Trees Could Talk*, I realized just how easy it was to put together a workbook. It's intended to be a place where you can explore the concepts and write down your answers to the questions that I've presented in this book. It has journal prompts, questions for you to reflect on, and plenty of space to get clear on your specific business blocks.

This work is of vital importance because, as you'll see throughout this book, I share plenty of examples of business blocks, but your blocks will, of course, be slightly different. They may have a different origin, or they may cause different problems in your business. They'll have a somewhat different essence than my blocks or the examples that I share from clients.

I also include in each chapter the links to relevant podcast episodes. I have over 300 episodes on my show, which first began in 2013, and there's so much relevant content there that will support your mindset journey. The episodes will shed light on your business blocks and help you to do this deep mindset work on your own.

I intend for this book to help you to get clear on your business blocks, so you can do the mindset work to release them. Sometimes the hardest part of doing mindset work is identifying our blocks. That's why I wrote this book: to make things easier for you. Only once you know what's blocking you in your business mindset can you do the work to shift your blocks and more easily move forward.

# INTRODUCTION TO THE FIRST EDITION

I'm so excited that you've started reading this book and are taking the first step to identify and release the blocks that are holding you back from creating the business of your dreams. I've been in business since 1999, and I know first hand what it's like to battle those inner gremlins that can hold us back from achieving our dreams. They can be crippling, keeping us stuck and frustrated in our business.

Sometimes they're obvious, sending us clear messages:

- You're not good enough!
- No one will pay what you're asking. What, are you crazy?
- You just need to take one more training course (or business course, or marketing course...the choices are endless), and *then* you'll know enough to start charging clients.
- Online marketing isn't for you...it's just too scary. Besides, you're not good at technology.
- No one will want what you have to offer. You're nothing special. It's been done before.

And sometimes they're not so obvious....

There are times when we aren't consciously aware of that negative mind chatter, but we are aware that there's something holding us back. Something that we can't quite put our finger on, because we don't even know what it is: we're just feeling stuck and frustrated and we want it to stop. When this happens, there might be limiting beliefs stuck deep in our subconscious mind, working on a level we can't easily access. We're talking about silent, invisible blocks, which may have been there your entire life, deep in your subconscious mind.

And this is what makes it frustrating: most of us aren't used to accessing our subconscious mind on a regular basis. It's not something our parents teach us, and it's certainly not something we learn in school or even university. It's the kind of thing you have to do special training to learn...*if* you're aware that such a thing is possible. Many people have no clue that this kind of thing is going on in their lives.

When we are able to access these fears, blocks, and limiting beliefs and get clear on exactly what's holding us back, or how we're self-sabotaging, then we know what we're working with. We know exactly what we need to change in our mindset, and from there it's just a matter of choosing *how* we want to transform those beliefs. Because, believe me, it's possible.

I know because I've done it. And I make it happen every day with my clients.

This book is a companion to my first book, *Business Beliefs*. It approaches business mindset from a slightly different angle and, like my first book, will help you identify which areas of your business mindset need to be upgraded the most. You can read the books in any order you like.

# 1

# PURPOSE OF THIS BOOK

"Nothing in life is to be feared, it is only to be understood. Now is the time to understand more, so that we may fear less."

— Marie Curie

I intend for this book to help you identify and overcome your business blocks. What are business blocks, you may wonder? They're the fears and limiting beliefs that hold you back from achieving your business goals and creating the business and lifestyle that you dream of.

When we struggle in our efforts to achieve our business goals and create our ideal business and life, the problem usually isn't that you need to learn more about business. That's easy enough—there's plenty of information and programs out there to teach you about entrepreneurship). On the contrary, it's usually the mindset stuff that's holding us back: fears, blocks, and limiting beliefs that make it difficult for us to take action toward our goals.

I discuss business beliefs in my first book, aptly titled *Business Beliefs: Upgrade Your Mindset to Overcome Self-Sabotage, Achieve Your Goals, and Transform Your Business (and Life)*. This book you have in your hands is designed to be a companion to *Business Beliefs*, which includes a list of over one thousand business belief statements. It also teaches you how to tap into your subconscious mind and identify which beliefs you hold at the subconscious level.

This book is simply a different way of looking at the stuff (I like to call it "mind crap") that's holding you back from creating your dream business. There are two more books in this series, both of which delve deeper into two fundamental aspects of business mindset: *Business Intuition* and *Business Visibility*. I think it's so easy to overlook the mindset stuff and just plod on, following the advice from the latest gurus and wondering why the results aren't showing up in terms of actual business results.

Looking at our business blocks involves a willingness to explore the shadow side of our mindset. That's why I chose the quote by Marie Curie to start the chapter. Sometimes we're afraid of exploring the shadow side of our thoughts and beliefs. But if we don't take a good look at our blocks, we'll never understand them, which means that we'll never be able to overcome them. You have to know where the obstacles are and what they look like before you can get over them.

But first things first... let's focus on *you* for a minute. And let's start with the end in mind. What exactly do you want to get out of reading this book? What are you hoping to achieve?

Stop reading for a minute, think about this, and then write down your answer somewhere. It's important to know what you want to get out of this book because it means you'll be more likely to achieve it. It's also essential to write it down, for three reasons:

1. It helps you clarify your intentions
2. It enables you to commit to these intentions
3. It helps you to see whether you have achieved these goals once you've finished reading this book and started working on your mindset.

Maybe you're new to the concept of changing your business mindset. Or perhaps you've got some experience working with your business mindset, but you're not sure where to go from here. Maybe you're aware that you've got some kind of block to achieving your business goals, but you can't quite put your finger on what they are.

In any case, this book of business blocks will help stimulate your exploration of what's holding you back from creating a successful, sustainable business and the lifestyle of your dreams. The deeper you dig to discover your blocks, the more likely you are to find the core of the issue that's stopping you from having that dream business today.

You're in the right place if:

- You're feeling frustrated with your business, and you know you need to do something differently.
- You've got a feeling that you might need to declutter your mind crap.
- You know your business mindset needs some upgrading to help you get your business to the next level.
- You're willing to take an honest look at what blocks might be holding you back.
- You're ready to take action to transform your business blocks.

Even though this is an expanded second edition, I've kept this book reasonably short, so you can use it as a quick, practical reference to uncover your business blocks, and not get caught up in lots of theory. I'm a big believer that *you* know what's best for you, so I encourage you to use this book in whatever way you find most useful.

## 2

# HOW TO USE THIS BOOK

> "My mother believed in curses, karma, good luck, bad luck, feng shui. Her amorphous set of beliefs showed me you can pick and choose the qualities of your philosophy, based on what works for you."
>
> — Amy Tan

I want you to use this book in whatever way feels right for *you*, which is why I selected the above quote to introduce the chapter. If you're new to the concept of identifying and releasing blocks, then you probably will want to read through each section before perusing the different categories of business blocks.

If you have any questions about the power of mindset, the power of beliefs, and the power of working with energy, I recommend you check out my first book, *Business Beliefs*. I debated about whether or not it would be useful to include those chapters in this book, but I didn't want to create too much overlapping content as I know a lot of people will buy both of these books—that's what happened with the first editions of these titles. Reading those chapters on mindset and beliefs will give you an idea of the importance of working at the deeper levels when transforming your mindset, and it will provide you with an introduction into beliefs and how they affect you.

*Business Beliefs* also includes a chapter on how to communicate with the subconscious mind, including several different techniques you can use on your own. You'll also find information on how to transform your beliefs and blocks at the "deeper" levels: the subconscious and energetic levels. It's certainly not necessary to read *Business Beliefs* before you read this book. Still, you may find it to be complementary to this one, and it will undoubtedly be a valuable part of your journey in transforming your mindset.

If you already have experience in a process or technique that works to change beliefs, you may want to skip straight to the chapters that explore the different categories of blocks. If you've purchased the ebook edition of this book, you might want to consider getting the print edition and also the workbook. While I love reading ebooks, as I said in the introduction, I find it most comfortable to read nonfiction in print. That way, I can underline passages and make notes in the margin—and then have the book on hand to use as a reference. One of my primary reasons for producing an updated, second edition of this book was so I could create the paperback edition.

The workbook includes some necessary information from this book, plus all of the journal prompts to help you explore your blocks and limiting beliefs so you can get clear on what you need to work on. It provides plenty of space for exploring your mindset, and it will help you to make this work even more profound.

The important thing is that you take the time to write

down your answers to the journal prompts, which will help you explore your blocks. If you simply read this book and then put it back on your bookshelf, you'll get nothing out of it. I want to make this absolutely clear: *You need to do the work.* This book is practical and useful, and it can spark a dramatic change in your mindset, but *only* if you do the work to change your mindset. Otherwise, it's nothing more than "shelf help."

If you have any questions, please get in touch via my website: www.hollyworton.com. I love hearing from readers.

3

## ABOUT ME

"Your intuition knows what to do. The trick is getting your head to shut up so you can hear."

— Louise Smith

For many years, I was a business mindset coach for women entrepreneurs. I worked with women who were feeling stuck and frustrated because they felt like they were hitting a plateau in their business. Maybe they were struggling to get a steady stream of clients, or perhaps they wanted to grow their business to a new level. My work was to help them release their fear of visibility, set aligned prices for their products and services, and take inspired action to grow their business.

Today, I've taken a step back from one-to-one sessions so I can focus on my writing. I've learned a lot from my years of coaching and mindset work with clients that I want to share in a more significant way through my books.

I'm dedicating this chapter to sharing my business journey with you so that I can clearly explain how changing my mindset has completely transformed my business and my life. That way, you'll understand *why* I do what I do: business mindset has been one of my biggest life lessons. My life—and business—can be divided into two phases:

1. Before I discovered mindset work
2. After I discovered mindset work

It's also crucial for me to tell you my story so you can get an idea of just how powerful it is to change your business mindset at the subconscious and energetic levels. I went from a place of having extremely low confidence and low self-esteem to being sure of myself and proud of what I do. Mindset work is profound work, and it can create significant results in very little time.

I know what it's like to struggle to build a business on my own. That's why I worked in the field of business mindset for so long. I know how it feels to be doing all the right things, and yet not achieve my goals. And I know what it's like to experience significant changes once I started doing the mindset work by transforming my beliefs at this profound level.

## My first company

I've been an entrepreneur since 1999. My first company, which was in the hospitality industry, was a constant uphill struggle as I learned new business and marketing skills. I was in a state of continual learning and expansion, which was both exciting and exhausting. I had quit my graduate studies in literature at UCLA to start the company with a business partner in Latin America.

Despite having zero experience in hospitality, my business partner and I managed to build a wildly successful business. We went from four small cabañas on the beach to owning and operating three ecological hotels in southeast Mexico, with a second property in development in Patagonia, and a central office in Buenos Aires that managed sales, reservations, and marketing.

Our hotels in Mexico were cutting edge: we were the first in the area to embrace and promote the concept of ecotravel, and we were the first to create a holistic spa featuring local Mayan healers and massage therapists. The resort was such a big part of our business that we used to say we had a "spa with hotels" rather than "three hotels with a spa."

We were a media darling. Editors from significant travel and spa publications came from all over the world to feature our properties. International celebrities came to stay with us—some returning for a second or third visit.

My primary role in the company was in the area of online marketing. We built our first website in 1999, and I soon started using pay-per-click advertising on Goto, which later became Overture and eventually Yahoo! Search Marketing (this was long before Google AdWords, or even Google, for that matter). Our marketing was also cutting edge compared to other hotels in the area. We fully embraced technology—despite being located in the jungle—and we focused our efforts on driving traffic directly to our website. We consistently brought more than 80% of our reservations, drastically reducing costs because we didn't have to pay much in travel agent commissions.

The business also spread and grew through word of mouth. One evening, I was hanging out near the front desk and asked a guest how they heard of us. To my surprise, he told me that he had been at a party in San Francisco and had met someone who had just returned from our hotel.

They were so effusive in their praise that the man went straight home and booked a stay with us.

We regularly heard from guests about how their lives had been changed by their holiday at our properties. Our seaside cabañas were candlelit, surrounded by native jungle, allowing guests to disconnect from their day to day hustle and enter a state of deep relaxation and recovery from stress. We had created something unique, and other hotels within the region began to copy us. These copycats were hoping to recreate our success.

It was both thrilling to receive such attention and attain such great success. It was also deeply satisfying to have created a unique experience that helped people in a significant way. However, there was another side to this phase of my life.

## The inner journey

My business partner and I were very different people, and we had very different skill sets and levels of entrepreneurial experience. For me, it was my first company, and for him, it was just one in a string of companies he had owned and operated. I threw myself into the operation of the business from the start, and I immediately felt out of place and overwhelmed with what I was doing. I felt very, very unqualified to be an entrepreneur.

I was learning new things on a daily basis, and I was implementing what I learned immediately after. Some aspects of the business I learned as a result of doing things the wrong way: I learned from my mistakes. It was 1999—the early days of the internet—so there wasn't as much information available then. It was a massive growth period for me, one that went on for the ten and a half years I ran the business with my partner.

The company was in a constant state of growth and expansion, and that meant the same for me. It was hugely transformative on a personal and professional level, but also incredibly frustrating and exhausting. I'm very grateful for the experience because I learned so much about business and marketing, but it was indeed a trial by fire.

Besides, my business partner and I had very different values, and he made decisions based on his values that regularly conflicted with my sense of integrity. I found myself in a position where I allowed him to make decisions for the business that felt entirely out of alignment for me.

## The shadow side

There was also a shadow side to this experience: my partner. My business partner wasn't a great person. I'm no psychiatrist, but he fits the profile of someone with narcissistic personality disorder. He was also a workaholic and demanded that I follow his example in working long and exhausting hours. He engaged in gaslighting, a tactic in which one person makes someone else question their reality, usually to gain control or power over them.

While I was busy at work co-creating and marketing this beautiful healing refuge for our guests, I also heard things like:

- *"You're so stupid. You're not even smart enough to be a secretary."*
- *"You're worthless."*
- *"You never do anything right. When anything goes wrong, you should just automatically apologize, because it's probably your fault, even if you think it's not."*

It was confusing because part of me knew that I was doing great work and getting great results in our business. The feedback I was getting from my business partner didn't correlate with the reality I was seeing. But because I heard things like this day in and day out, over the course of ten years, I started to lose touch with reality. I began to question what I was seeing. I stopped trusting myself, and I began to believe the things I heard at a very deep level.

These statements, and many others like them, seeped into my subconscious mind and adversely affected my beliefs. They set me up with a mindset that would negatively affect my future business ventures and make it very, very difficult for me to build a successful business on my own. It's been over a decade since I left that partnership, and I've taken that long to undo the damage. I'm still working on my healing. This stuff went in deep.

## The disconnect deepened

Eventually, I became so disconnected from myself that I had no idea which way was up, in terms of my internal compass. The gaslighting had me completely disoriented. So many things felt wrong, and I felt so lost that I didn't know how to get myself out of the mess I had created for myself.

Ten and a half years later, when I quit running the company, I was so lost and out of touch with myself that I didn't know what I wanted. All I knew was that I couldn't take it anymore. I no longer wanted to be running a business with my partner, even though I dearly loved the people who worked for us, and I felt terrible about abandoning them, which was how I saw it at the time.

## A new beginning

Eventually, I left. In 2008 I moved out, and almost a year later, I quit the business. It was one of the hardest decisions I'd ever had to make. I had co-created the company from scratch, and I genuinely cared about the business and the people who worked there. But I knew it had to be done, for my own mental and emotional wellbeing.

Around the time I left my company in 2009, I met my husband. With his help, I started to realize I wasn't the stupid, useless person I believed myself to be. I also began to understand just how bad things had been for the past ten years of my life. I had lost all perspective on how I deserved to be treated by others.

After quitting my first company, I took an extended sabbatical, which ended up lasting almost a year and a half. I took time off to heal, rest, and recover. I also spent the time trying to figure out what I wanted to do next. I knew I had lots of skills, but I wasn't sure what to do with them.

Near the end of the sabbatical, we packed up everything and moved to London, where I trained as a coach and as an NLP (Neuro-Linguistic Programming) practitioner. I was so excited to run a business where I could help people once again, albeit in a very different way. I was very enthusiastic about my new skills, and I was confident that I was on the right path.

I started with a life coaching business, helping women to find their life purpose. It was tough, and I struggled to get clients, despite knowing what I needed to do to start a business. Out of all the other coaches I trained with, I was the only one who had a decade of practical business and online marketing experience. I knew what to do, and I was putting it into action, but for some reason, my company just wasn't working.

After several months of struggle, I heeded the advice of a business mentor. I settled into a social media marketing company, where I used the skills in online marketing that I learned in my very first company to help authors learn to use social media for marketing their books online. This business later evolved into helping women solopreneurs with social media. But it still wasn't easy.

## The struggle

I was making enough money to support myself and to pay the bills, but it was a constant struggle. Building my business was *so damn hard*. There was no sense of ease and flow. It was all push, push, push to get minimal results. It was exhausting and disheartening.

If my first business was a lesson in practical business and marketing skills, my solopreneur adventures have been a lesson in business mindset. In Tribal Publishing and Socially Holistic, the names of my social media companies, I learned for the first time about the *other* kind of struggle that happens in business—the one that very few people discuss. (Tribal Publishing started out providing social media services and consulting for authors and only later evolved into what it is today: my own publishing company, which also provides publishing services to authors.)

In my new companies, I was no longer part of a large organization; I was a solopreneur, and my company was all about *me*. I didn't have the confidence to step into my greatness and shine brightly with my new business endeavors.

On the contrary: I shrank into the shadows, crippled by my smallness. It felt like I was taking one step forward and two steps backward with my marketing. I was trying to put myself out there, but *not too much*. I was playing it safe—safe inside my comfort zone.

For the first time in my life, I battled my inner mindset gremlins—lack of confidence and low self-esteem—as I struggled to build my social media business and get clients. New fears, blocks, and limiting beliefs reared their ugly heads daily. I believed I wasn't good enough, and that I wasn't worthy of having a successful business. It felt crippling.

And the worst part of it was that I had no idea what was going on. I just thought that I needed to take yet another online marketing course (despite having ten years of experience in the area) or hire another coach or business mentor (despite already knowing what I needed to do). I believed those things would fix all my problems. I struggled, and I pushed, and I put in so much effort, but I didn't get much in terms of results.

### A light in the darkness

I was entirely in the dark about what was going on: that my mindset didn't serve me one bit. It was full of fears and blocks and limiting beliefs that kept me stuck. I was also struggling with personal issues that weren't shifting no matter what therapies I tried.

A friend of mine eventually recommended that I train in a process that he was using with his clients: PSYCH-K®. This process helped me to quickly and easily change my subconscious beliefs. It was a simple process that helped me to easily communicate with my subconscious mind so I could change the beliefs that limited my self-esteem, my relationships, my business performance, and even my physical health. I used it to transform *every single aspect of my life*.

I started where everyone starts: with the Basic Workshop, and I used the process daily with myself. The results were so quick and precise that I attended the Advanced Integration Workshop, and later the Pro (which has since evolved into the Master Facilitation Workshop). Not wanting to miss a single workshop, I traveled to the US to attend the Health and Wellbeing Program, which completely transformed my physical health and wellness.

When I find something that works, I throw myself into it completely. After using this process regularly for over a year, I went back and did all the training *again.* This time, I was able to absorb the little details that made much more sense after more than a year of working with this process regularly. It deepened my understanding of beliefs and how I worked with them, and it made me a much better facilitator. I was settling into my mindset work, both with myself and with clients.

**Big life changes**

This process was life-changing. It lifted me from a place of stuckness and struggle and transported me into a place of ease and flow. The more I used it, the easier things became.

My mindset dramatically shifted to a more positive, uplifting state. Tasks that I had previously procrastinated on suddenly became easy to complete. Working through my to-do list became easy, rather than a constant struggle. Reaching out to joint venture partners, something which used to terrify me, was instantly simple. Setting up Facebook ads to reach a larger audience, something I used to balk at, became easy. Being visible in my business felt natural, rather than terrifying.

I know this sounds too good to be true, but here's what was happening: I was no longer sabotaging my efforts. That alone made everything so much easier. So many of the things that used to hold me back became easy to take action on. And as a result of taking these actions, my business grew, and it was easier to get clients to sign up for my products and services. Things started to flow with ease.

This process was so hugely transformational for me and my business that I knew I had to start using it to help others. I added it to Socially Holistic, my social media company because so many of the women I worked with had inner struggles around their online marketing. They either believed they weren't tech-savvy, or else they were afraid of being visible online in a big way. Or both. I used to say that I helped people with social media from the inside and out. Not only did I teach them practical techniques and strategy, but I also helped them to release the blocks that kept them from using this strategy so they could step up in a more significant way.

The more I worked with women on the inner side of online marketing, the more I realized that this mindset work was my favorite part of my business. It was the most fulfilling part of my work, and I decided it was time for me to transform my business once again. It was a big decision, but I was confident that I was on the right path.

## Big business changes

I decided to let go of the technical aspect of Socially Holistic and revisit a brand I had built a few years back when I first trained as a coach: Ready to Bloom. I had always loved the name, and it perfectly fit the work I was doing: helping women solopreneurs transform their business mindset so their business could bloom. I wanted to help as many entrepreneurs to be successful in their businesses as I possibly could.

In 2016, I rebranded once again and let go of the Ready to Bloom brand. As much as I loved the name, I felt that it was time for me to stop hiding behind a business name and step up into my personal brand. I was the central part of my business and the work that I did, and it was time to make that apparent through my business name. I'm positive that it was my mindset work that led me to this point. It had once felt safe to hide behind a business brand, while now it felt limiting. It was time to step up and *just be me.*

Interestingly, this decision came just one month after I released the first edition of this book. Writing and publishing my first business mindset book was yet another significant step in terms of business visibility and claiming my spot as an expert in the field of business mindset. It was a big, scary step, and it triggered lots of hidden limiting beliefs for me to work on.

"Who are you to write a book about business mindset?" demanded my mind gremlins. But I did the mindset work, I released the fears and limiting beliefs, and the book went out. Since then, I've written and published another eight books and one workbook.

And I've continued to grow from there, not just as a writer but as an author-entrepreneur.

**Heart-centered Energy Work®**

In late April 2016, about the same time, I was rebranding my entire business, I received a message from my spirit guides via my business mentor, Lisa Wechtenhiser. Spirit guides are energetic beings that include angels, ascended masters, ancestors, elementals, and spirit animals or power animals. Essentially, they're spirits that have the ability and desire to help us and guide us in life.

Lisa calls herself the "trust whisperer," and she's been an essential part of my journey to stepping into my power and trusting my intuition. She's helped me to step up in a much bigger way. I come away from each session with her with lists of mindset work to do on my own. Lisa also calls herself "practically woo" because she channels your guides as she delivers practical business advice. This two-pronged approach to business is super powerful.

In this particular session, the guides chimed in to inform me that I was experiencing a significant upgrade, like a door opening. They told me that I was about to experience a shift in terms of what I did and how I helped people to transform their mindset. They urged me to make a list of which aspects of PSYCH-K® felt right to me, and which parts didn't.

They asked me to look at what I most resonated with, and what wasn't me. The guides suggested I explore how I currently blended these things, and to consider whether maybe there was a new way to do my work. They said that it was time for me to find what that worked for me—something new.

The spirit guides told me that I needed to create my process. They asked me to put together a list of ingredients and to metaphorically put them into a mixing bowl and stir them up. They said that the process I would eventually use with clients would look very different.

They were right. I went away and made my lists, and I spent most of 2016 with the plan to create a new process. I intuitively knew that it would be something that I would receive as a kind of information download and not something that I would create rationally. And so I waited for it to happen.

And I waited.

It was a long process, and there was a bit of struggle, mainly because I simply didn't make the time and space for it to come through. But eventually, in late 2016, over the course of just five days, I channeled the new technique that

I later used to help clients with their business mindset. It's called Heart-centered Energy Work®, and it helps to not only transform beliefs at the subconscious level but also to release any energy blocks at the same time.

It's quick and powerful, and it gets excellent results for both my clients and me. The critical point for me to make here is that I would never have been able to channel this profoundly transformative technique if I hadn't done the mindset work to get myself to a place where I believed I could do it. I believed in myself, and I knew I had the power to receive this information, but only because I had previously done the mindset work to reprogram my beliefs.

### Author-entrepreneur

And then, in late 2018, I decided to quit my business mindset work to focus on my writing. This change felt like a risky move. I worried that people wouldn't take me seriously. I stressed that people would think I was flaky—yet again. But I knew that I loved writing, and I wanted to focus my work on helping a wider audience. That would be much easier to do by writing books, rather than filling my calendar with one-to-one sessions.

I've been there

As you can see, I've come from a challenging place: one of extreme lack of self -belief and self-confidence. I know what it's like to feel frustrated not to have all the necessary pieces to have your business work. I know what it's like to focus on the practical side of the business and to ignore the mindset work completely. I know what it's like to struggle. And I've come out the other side.

That's why it was so vital for me to tell you my full story: so you could see how far I've come in just a few years. I ran my first business from 1999 to 2009 and started my coaching journey in 2011. It wasn't until mid-2013 that I started to focus on my mindset—that's less than three years before I released the first edition of this book.

That's not much time, considering how far I've come in terms of mindset. I went from being in a very, very dark place to release my smallness and stepping into my greatness. I let go of the mind crap that was holding me back, and I adopted new beliefs that served me better.

And then it all came together: my coaching training from back in 2011 has helped me to help my clients dig deep and to get clear on what's currently holding them back and what they want instead, so we can start transforming those beliefs quickly and effectively. My work with authors in my first social media business in 2012 has given me the tools and knowledge to help people through my books, such as this one. And my extensive mindset work, which I began in 2013, got me to the place where I believed in myself.

This process all sounds straightforward in retrospect because I can now look back on the past few years and see how it's all come together seamlessly. But there were some murky bits, which I hope that I clearly expressed when telling my story because I believe that it's essential to look at the shadow side of things. The deeper we dig, the more valuable the treasure we will find.

When I speak of treasure, I'm referring to two things: first, the core limiting beliefs that, once shifted, will unlock and transform all the other limiting beliefs that hover near the surface and are often easier to spot. One of my PSYCH-K® instructors called this "finding the diamond." We can work much more quickly when we're willing to dig deep within ourselves to get to the root of an issue.

The second part of the treasure is clarity. A lot of my work—first with one-to-one clients, now with my books—involves helping people get clarity on exactly what it is that they *do* want so that we can program that intention into their subconscious. Once you have a clear vision for your business, and once you believe that you're capable of achieving this vision, the easier it will be for you to take practical action to make it happen.

Now that I've shared my business journey with you and you can see the power of mindset work, we're ready to talk about the power of beliefs, the power of the subconscious mind, and the power of energy work. Because that's where we often get stuck, and that's where the real magic can happen, once we know how to do the work and get out of our way.

**Take action today**

Before we get into the next chapter, I'd like to encourage you to write down *your* story. Start wherever you want: you can begin with your first job in high school, or your lemonade stand as a child (I had an orange juice stand). Get into the details when you relate your business journey: what were all the different iterations of your business? What did you do? How did you help people?

Most importantly, how did you *feel* at all the different stages of your entrepreneurial journey? Were you afraid people would find out you were a fraud? Were you afraid you weren't good enough? Did you always compare yourself to other entrepreneurs with a similar business model? What were your fears and beliefs about yourself and about your ability to run a successful business? What are your current fears and beliefs?

4

# THE POWER OF THE SUBCONSCIOUS MIND

"We never stop to consider that our beliefs are only a relative truth that's always going to be distorted by all the knowledge we have stored in our memory."

— Miguel Ángel Ruiz

Let's talk a little bit about the subconscious, also known in the field of psychoanalysis as the unconscious mind. French psychologist Pierre Janet coined the term "subconscious," which is the anglicized version of the French word *subconscient*. The 18th-century German Romantic philosopher Friedrich Schelling coined the term "unconscious mind," which was later introduced into English by poet and essayist Samuel Taylor Coleridge. It was eventually popularized by Austrian psychoanalyst Sigmund Freud, who saw the mind as being comprised of three levels:

- the conscious (10 percent of total brain function)

- the subconscious (50–60 percent)
- the unconscious (30–40 percent).

Modern-day representations of the conscious and the subconscious/unconscious minds will put the breakdown at 10–12 percent for the conscious mind and 88–90 percent for the subconscious/unconscious mind. For this book, all we need to know is that roughly 90% of total brain function does *not* take place in the conscious mind. This concept is fundamental.

You may have seen the use of an iceberg as a metaphor for the subconscious mind: just the tip of it is visible above the water, with the vast majority of the iceberg being invisible, submerged. The visible section represents your conscious mind, with the submerged part representing your subconscious mind because it is unseen, operating in the background. It's like a foundation for the conscious mind, which metaphorically sits on the surface.

Let's dig a bit deeper into the two. We'll also explore a concept known as the superconscious mind, which you may or may not be familiar with.

**The conscious mind**

This is the part of your mind that you're aware of throughout the day. You use it to envision what you want for your company, and you use it to set your business and life goals, to make decisions, and to plan your day. It's where logic and intellect reside, as well as your short term memory. Critical thinking skills are a part of the conscious mind, which you use to think abstractly and judge results. A big part of running your business happens in the conscious mind.

The conscious mind is time-bound and has an awareness of the past and the future. It is also said to have a minimal processing capacity: it can only focus on one to three events at a time. Again, the conscious mind makes up only about 10 percent of your total brain function.

### The subconscious mind

The subconscious mind is the other 90 percent. It's responsible for all of your involuntary physical functions, such as breathing and walking. It monitors the operation of your entire body: it keeps your motor functions operating, it keeps your heart going, it makes your digestive system work, and it carries out all of the functions of your body. Take breathing. For example, you do not think about when to inhale and exhale; your subconscious mind handles that for you.

In addition to handling our essential body functions, the subconscious also handles the parts of the mind that we are not fully aware of, but which influence our actions, feelings, and emotions. It is responsible for our habits and patterns. Because the subconscious handles our long-term memory, it's in charge of storing all of our life experiences. It holds our past events, our attitudes, our beliefs, our values.

The subconscious mind is said to think literally. When you are communicating with it (you'll learn how to do that in a later chapter), you need to be crystal clear on what exactly it is that you want. The subconscious is in some ways like a small child: it takes everything you say to the letter. If you are familiar with the law of attraction, you may be aware of this concept: you need to be very specific about what you want so you can communicate the right message to the subconscious mind.

The subconscious mind is also timeless: it exists in the

now. Because it only deals in the present time, it has no sense of past or future. If you work with affirmations or belief statements, they need to be in the present tense.

They also need to be positive statements, as the subconscious does not process negative commands. If you try to program a belief such as "I don't get myself into debt," the subconscious will ignore the "don't" and instead will hear "I get myself into debt." Think about it this way: if you're in London and you want to visit Covent Garden, you won't get good results by walking up to someone and saying "Please don't give me directions to Buckingham Palace." You'd want to specifically ask for directions on how to get to Covent Garden because that's where you want to go. Focus on what you do want, not on what you don't want.

Our subconscious is also responsible for our self-sabotage. It has all this information based on our life experiences stored in its long term memory, and it's in charge of self-preservation. This means that—based on the beliefs it holds—it can sometimes make somewhat illogical decisions or lead us to take irrational action in its effort to keep us safe and secure.

While this can be incredibly frustrating, it's important to remember that our subconscious is merely trying to help. If a person "accidentally" misses a deadline to apply for a speaking engagement, that might simply have been their subconscious trying to help them avoid public humiliation. Like when they stood up in front of the class in fifth grade to give a presentation and then tripped and fell, causing the entire class to burst out in laughter.

The subconscious mind is a powerhouse: it does so much, and it does it automatically, working in the background. It is not something that we usually control. However, it is something that we *can* control: instead of falling victim to the often unhelpful guidance of our subconscious, which may be operating on old programs, we have ways of programming new beliefs into the subconscious.

When I talk about "deep mindset work," this is what I mean: reprogramming new beliefs into our subconscious. This process is how I work with myself and with other people to transform beliefs and mindset. Unfortunately, most people are unfamiliar with these types of techniques, and therefore this is something that they do not do on a day to day basis. Most of us function with the subconscious running its programs automatically, even when they no longer serve us.

## The superconscious mind

Some spiritual belief systems acknowledge a third part of the mind, known as the superconscious or higher self. You may know this by another term, such as the authentic self, the divine self, the higher mind, universal consciousness, or the soul. If you don't believe in this concept, that's fine, and you can move right along to the next section. I need to address this, but you don't have to believe in it yourself. You'll still get the results from working with your subconscious mind.

The superconscious mind, or higher self, is the core of who you are as an individual. It knows your path to success, your life purpose, your life passion. It knows where you've come from and where you're going. It's in charge of delivering wise guidance to you in the form of your intuition or gut feeling. If you believe in a higher power, you may see it as being your connection with the Divine, Source, Spirit, God, Goddess, or whatever you call this spiritual power.

The superconscious can also be accessed to get wisdom

regarding our mindset and the beliefs that we need to have to achieve our goals—more on that in a bit.

### Take action today

What are your thoughts about all this? Take a few minutes to think about—or to journal on—your current relationship with your conscious, subconscious, and superconscious minds. Are you truly in touch with each aspect of yourself? Do you feel better connected to one part of your mind than to the others? Do you believe in the concept of the superconscious mind? If so, what do you call it?

### On the podcast

You can find the full list of podcast episodes here:
www.hollyworton.com/podcast

- • 272 Holly Worton ~ Mindset: Why It Isn't About Positive Thinking

## 5

# THE NEFARIOUS POWER OF BLOCKS

"You can't just declare that you have a growth mindset. Growth mindset is hard."

— Carol S. Dweck

As I said at the end of the last chapter, you need to do the work to transform your mindset. It doesn't happen on its own, no matter how much you engage in positive thinking. That's why I chose the above quote to introduce this chapter. I don't think that having a growth mindset is *hard*, but I do believe it takes *work*. Again, not necessarily *hard* work, but you certainly need to put both time and effort into transforming your mindset.

This chapter title may sound a bit dramatic, but let's face it: business blocks can be hard to uncover if we don't have any guidance or system for doing so. And most people (unfortunately) don't have a way to access their blocks easily. This process is something that I developed over the course of several years, and it's a combination of things I learned through training in various processes and techniques and also through practical experience with transforming my mindset and helping clients transform theirs.

When your subconscious mind is on board with your conscious vision for your business and lifestyle, all is well. It's easy to take action and achieve your goals. But when your subconscious *isn't* on board, that's a whole different story: that's when your day to day life is full of fears, blocks, and limiting beliefs that hold you back from taking action toward your business goals.

Have you ever felt totally stuck in your business? Maybe you've been taking action, following the advice of the latest business gurus, or working with a business coach or mentor. Or perhaps you've been stuck, procrastinating on your to-do list and spending your days wasting time on social media when you could be using it to market your business. I think we've all been there at one point or another. It's rough.

Either way, something isn't working. Maybe the business guru's advice isn't aligned with your own beliefs and style, so your efforts come across as awkward to your followers. And if you're wasting time on social media, well ...that's just time that you've lost, and deep down, you know it. And it doesn't feel right.

It's what we often refer to as self-sabotage, although I always hesitate to call it that—you aren't sabotaging yourself. Instead, your subconscious mind is trying to keep you safe within your comfort zone. It's got your best interests in mind—kind of. On the one hand, it wants you to be safe; on the other hand, many of the actions we need to take to create our dream business take us *outside* our comfort zone. When our subconscious is "sabotaging" us, it can lead to procrastination and feeling stuck and frustrated in business.

That's why it's so essential to understand precisely what

your business blocks are: so you can identify them and transform them. Toward the end of this book, I'll talk about how you can change your business blocks into business bliss. There are many options for releasing blocks at the subconscious level, and you need to find the right process or technique for you.

This book is complementary to my *Business Beliefs* book. You don't have to read them in any particular order, but they work together to help you uncover your current mindset, including your current fears, blocks, and limiting beliefs. Start with one of the books, do the mindset work on what you've uncovered, and then work through the second book to go even deeper.

For now, we're going to take a look at how to discover your business blocks. Then we'll make it even more in-depth by going through a list of fifteen different categories so we can get to the root of all the various business blocks you may be experiencing. It's essential to be open and curious about this: try to accept your blocks, rather than reject them or repress them. Don't be ashamed of them, and don't be alarmed—your blocks are easy to change, but before you can change them, you have to know precisely what they are.

Sometimes we tend to pretend these blocks don't exist or to sweep them under the rug. If we do that, they won't go away. They'll just be buried deeper and deeper into our subconscious minds, where they will continue to do damage. Only it will be more challenging to do something about them.

The point of this book is to dig up the "mind crap," take a look at it, and then use this valuable information to transform the blocks into bliss. It can be done, and it's not as hard as it sounds. In fact, it can be easy and effortless. But first, you've got to do the detective work. In the same way that *Business Beliefs* was about bringing to light the positive beliefs that will enhance our lives and our business, this book is about uncovering the shadow side of our mindset. It's essential to do both kinds of work.

Are you with me? I promise I'll try to make this as painless and as uplifting as possible. However, *you'll still need to do the work yourself.* Have I made that clear yet?

6

# THE HORRIBLE POWER OF FEARS

"...my fear wants me to be safe, and my fear perceives all motion, all inspiration, all work, all activity, all passion whatsoever as potentially life-threatening. My fear wants me to live a smaller life. The smallest imaginable life, ideally. My fear would prefer that I never got out of bed."

— Elizabeth Gilbert

What is fear? It's an unpleasant and uncomfortable emotion caused by the perceived threat of danger, pain, or harm. It's a very natural emotion, and fear can be critical to our survival. Fear can be useful to us, and it can also hinder our growth and development...if we allow it to do so. There are two main types of fear: rational fear (we're out on a hike, and as we come around a bend we see a bear) and irrational fear (we avoid making a decision in our business because we're afraid we'll end up bankrupt and homeless). The first example is a situation when we're facing real-life danger, and the second is a perceived fear that may or may not occur. These perceived threats or fears are just another type of business block.

Fear usually causes us to react in one of four main ways: fight, flight, freeze, and fawn. However, we can also respond with a combination of these patterns. We may react in one way to one type of fear or conflict, and we may respond in a completely different way in another kind of situation.

## Fight

This is pretty self-explanatory: it means that we respond by aggressively confronting the threat. In this type of reaction, we may feel tense, our jaw tight, our teeth clenched. We may feel intense anger like we want to punch or kick someone or something. We may even cry.

An entrepreneur who tends to fight may bully their business partner or their employees. They may attempt to damage the reputation of the other person or blame someone else to "win" the conflict. If an employee attempts to quit their job and leave the company, a fight-inclined business owner may try to coerce them into staying. Or the entrepreneur may attack a particular project and its supporters or the team involved—to the extent that they may even sabotage the project.

## Flight

The exact opposite response: it means that we run away from the threat. We may feel restless and fidgety, even though we don't physically run away. We may feel trapped and tense, ready for takeoff.

A business owner who tends flight may ignore any conflict that occurs—or, worse, they may disappear altogether, not answering emails, phone calls, or other communication. In going radio silent, they avoid the situation entirely. Or they may remain present in the office, busying themselves with unimportant admin work so they can avoid the situation without anyone noticing.

### Freeze

In this scenario, we find ourselves unable to fight or flight. We seem to have lost the ability to move or act in response to the threat. We may feel numb, though our heart is pounding. We may feel a sense of dread.

An entrepreneur who tends to freeze is the kind of person who does nothing in the face of fear. This is a passive response to conflict. They may, for example, avoid innovation in their field because they want to wait and see how things will turn out in their industry before taking action.

### Fawn

The least well-known of the four, this response is often referred to as "people-pleasing." It's when we comply with the threatening person or accommodate their needs to save ourselves, and it's a typical response in abusive relationships. In fact, "fawn" is a term that was coined by Pete Walker, a C-PTSD (complex post-traumatic stress disorder) survivor and licensed therapist who specializes in helping adults who experienced childhood trauma.

Business owners who tend to fawn may be big people pleasers who struggle in their relationships with clients. They may avoid setting and upholding boundaries. They may feel taken advantage of by their business partner because they say "yes" to every request and suggestion that their partner makes, even if they don't agree with them. They want to avoid conflict.

## Uncovering our fears

Fear is uncomfortable. Some people tend to sweep their fears under the rug, so they don't have to look at them. Unfortunately, even though the fears have been suppressed and hidden, they haven't gone away, and they're still operating in the background, affecting the person's actions and decisions.

That's why it's so important to take a look at our fears. They're just as easy to transform as other types of business blocks, but we can't do the work to release our fears until we identify what they are. There's nothing wrong or shameful about having business-related fears; we all have them.

Before we delve into the fifteen categories of business blocks (and fears), let's get clear on what we want in our business and our life. This is one excellent way to bring fears to the surface so we can release them.

# 7

# GET CLEAR ON WHAT YOU WANT

"When you know what you want, and want it bad enough, you will find a way to get it."

— Jim Rohn

First, you need to know what you want. Are you 100% clear on the vision you have for your business and life? How do you want to step into your greatness and become a leader in your field? What do you want to experience in your business and life?

Back in 2015, I did a podcast episode on How to Get Clear on Your Big Business Vision (find it here: www.hollyworton.com/111/), which includes a guided meditation and a worksheet that walks you through each stage of this process to help you get clear on exactly what you want for your business. On that page, you can also find links to download both the meditation and also a pdf with these questions so that you can write them out.

I highly recommend that you print out this list or write the answers down in your journal (or get the workbook edition of this book, which has plenty of room to write down your answers). This is essential information that will help you to determine what you need to believe to make your dream a reality.

**Visual**

Let's imagine that you've fully stepped into your greatness and that you're living your big vision for your business and life.

- What does stepping into your greatness mean to you?
- What does that look like?
- What do you see yourself doing?
- How do you see yourself starting your day? What time do you get up? Do you set an alarm, or do you wake up naturally?
- What does your morning ritual look like? How long does it last?
- What do you eat/drink in the morning?
- What do you do once your morning routine is over?
- What time do you start working?
- Do you work from home, or do you leave home to work? What does your office or workspace look like?
- What do you work on? Your own creative projects? Do you do work for clients or with clients?
- If you're working with clients, what does this look like? Envision yourself with one of these ideal clients.
- Are you writing, creating art, or content for your

business? Envision yourself doing whatever it is that you'll be doing once you've achieved this goal of your ideal business.

- Take a look at your bank account. Either look at your bank statement, or access your account on your computer. Now that you've got your ideal business, how much money is in your checking/current account? And how much do you have in savings? How much do you have in investments and in your pension/retirement fund?
- What does the rest of your day look like?
- What do you eat/drink throughout the day?
- What else do you do throughout the afternoon?
- What time do you wrap up your work or creative activities?
- What does your lifestyle look like? What else are you doing in your life, when you're not working directly on your business? What do you see yourself doing?
- What do you see yourself doing for exercise/fitness? What time of the day do you exercise?
- Where do you see yourself living? What country are you in? What city, town, or village? Is it an urban environment, or is it rural?
- What does your home look like?
- What does your evening or nighttime routine look like? How long does it last?
- Is there anything else you need to look at to give you a clear vision of what things look like now you are living the life of your dreams? Take a few seconds to look at that.
- As you reflect on your day, you see how your

ideal day is different from your current lifestyle. What are some other things that are different?

**Auditory**

- Once you've fully stepped into your greatness, what will you be saying to yourself? It could be: "I'm proud of myself," "I can't believe I did this," "I'm so happy that I made it," or something else.
- What will you hear other people saying about you? It could be: "She's amazing," "Wow, I can't believe what she's done with her business," or something else.
- What are your clients saying about you?
- What else do you hear in your life, now that you've fully stepped into your greatness? What's going on in the background as you live your day? Do you hear children? Pets? Birds? Music? Other people?
- Is your home in a quiet area, or is it bustling and active? What about your office or workplace?

**Kinesthetic**

- How do you feel when you wake up in the morning?
- How do you feel throughout the day? What are your energy levels like? What emotions are you feeling?
- How do you feel in the evening as you're getting ready for bed?
- Now that you've fully stepped into your

greatness, how do you feel? Are you feeling free? Satisfied? Proud of yourself? Excited about the future? Write down *all the things* you feel.
- What are you grateful for in your ideal lifestyle?

### Dial it up

Often, our beliefs limit our vision for ourselves. Read through your answers and mark any details where you're playing small or hesitating to dream big. Dial up the intensity and the bigness of your vision: how can you make it better, more exciting, or more satisfying? No one else has to see this but you, so don't be afraid to make your dream bigger, better, and bolder.

As you dial up the intensity of this vision, pay attention to any fears or limiting beliefs that you have, and write those down. What fears do you have about living this ideal lifestyle? What will people think of you? Will you lose family or friends with this lifestyle change? What will they say about you? Do you believe you're worthy of having this dream? Are you deserving of living this life of your dreams? Write down all the "yes, buts".

### Repeat

You can repeat this visualization or this process as many times as you like. You may want to repeat it every quarter, so you can get clarity on how your vision has grown and changed over the previous months. As we grow, our vision for our business changes and we need to understand precisely how our ideal business vision changes over time so we can adjust our goals, strategy, and business plan accordingly.

I've been talking a lot lately about stepping into your

greatness, and when we're not in a good place, it can be hard to tap into our greatness and see what it is. So give yourself permission to dream big and to repeat this process regularly, so you can gradually step up your vision of what you want for your business and your life. Each time, you'll expand your vision of what's possible for your business and life.

### Action plan

- What are the top three actions you could take this week to bring you closer to stepping into your greatness?
- Who do you need to be to take these actions?
- What do you need to believe about yourself to take these actions easily?
- What might stop you from taking these actions? What would you rather have instead? How would you rather feel about your action plan? What do you need to do/experience instead? What do you need to believe about yourself and your ability to complete this action plan?

### Business beliefs

- Who do you need to be to step into your greatness fully? Who do you need to be to achieve your big business vision?
- What do you need to believe about yourself to step into your greatness fully?
- What's stopping you from stepping into your

greatness? What would you rather have instead? What do you need to do/experience instead?

**Wrap it up**

Is there anything else you need to add to the vision? Are there any specific goals that you need to add that you want to achieve as part of your vision for stepping into your greatness? Get it all out and into words that you can see. That will make it easier for you to identify specific beliefs in the lists that follow.

**Take action today**

If you haven't already, answer the questions that I've posed for you in this chapter. They'll help you dig up fears and limiting beliefs for you to work on. Then decide when you want to revisit these questions and put it in the calendar, so you remember to do it.

**On the podcast**

You can find the full list of podcast episodes here:
www.hollyworton.com/podcast

- 195 Holly Worton ~ How to Stay Grounded + Strong in Your Vision
- 111 Holly Worton ~ How to Get Clear on Your Big Business Vision

# 8

# HOW TO DISCOVER YOUR BUSINESS BLOCKS

"Life is very, very simple and easy to understand, but we complicate it with the beliefs and ideas that we create."

— Don Miguel Ruiz

It can be challenging to discover your blocks, especially if this is something you're not used to paying attention to. This book will help you to do a scan of all your business blocks in different aspects of your business (and life, because everything is connected). You can go through this book and uncover your blocks regularly. And in the process of doing this work, you'll retrain your mind to see the blocks more quickly and easily, so you can get to work on releasing them right away.

As I mentioned earlier, I designed this to be a companion to my first book, *Business Beliefs: Upgrade Your Mindset to Overcome Self-Sabotage, Achieve Your Goals, and Transform Your Business (and Life)*. This book you've got in your hands takes the fifteen categories of beliefs from *Business Beliefs* and explores them from a different angle. Each chapter contains a brief introduction to the category, and then explores business blocks in that category from four perspectives:

1. Symptoms of blocks, to help you see how they show up in real life
2. Fears, which are another type of blocks
3. Questions about potential blocks, to help you discover your specific blocks
4. Examples of other people's blocks, which will help you uncover your own

### Symptoms of blocks

The section describing symptoms of blocks gives several examples of ways that these blocks may show up in your business. You may experience one, some, or all of these symptoms...or perhaps none. You might not have blocks in every single category of this book, or the examples provided might spark your memory of other ways these blocks have shown up in your business. If so, make a note of them.

### Fears

Fears are just another type of business block, and this section lists several fears related to each category. As always, you may resonate with some, but not all. Others may trigger an awareness of fears that you had previously never noticed. Be sure to make a note of everything. Fears are just as easy to shift as other types of business blocks.

### Discover your blocks

The following section asks you several questions to help you dig deeper and uncover what's going on around those blocks. Some of them may apply to you; others may not. But they might trigger the discovery of other, related blocks. Be sure to write these down.

What else is happening for you? What's stopping you from overcoming these blocks? You might want to make notes to answer these questions, or you might want to pull out a journal or notebook and write a more in-depth answer to the questions. You could also write them down in a file on your computer or phone. Or you can get the companion workbook, which will help you to keep everything together in one place. Go with whatever works for you. But be sure to get them out of your head and onto paper (or on your computer). Otherwise, it's far too easy to forget them.

### Examples of blocks

The final section in each chapter includes examples of what these blocks might look like for you. You might resonate with these, or they might spark your imagination and help you uncover specific blocks of your own in each category. Often, hearing someone else's story will trigger an understanding of what's blocking you.

### Peeling the onion

This work is kind of like peeling off the layers of an onion: you'll be able to identify many business blocks on your first read-through of this book. Once you've got clarity on your blocks and have done the work to release them at the subconscious level, others may rise to the surface. Sometimes it can feel like the onion is infinite. Still, if you read this book, and you do the transformation work regularly, you can radically transform your business mindset at a profound level. You will see changes in your business and life.

You may also find that, as you grow your business to new levels, you'll encounter new business blocks. As you step into your business in a more significant way, you'll face new, different situations that may trigger fears that hadn't yet come to the surface. This provides you with new opportunities to identify and transform new fears, blocks, and limiting beliefs.

This work isn't something you need to do daily. But the more you work on discovering and transforming your business blocks, the faster you will upgrade your business mindset, and the easier it will become to take action on the things you've been procrastinating on. When I first trained in PSYCH-K®, I was so excited about having the power to quickly and easily transform my beliefs at the subconscious level that I worked on changing between ten and twenty beliefs daily. I did it by keeping a list of everything that came up for me during the day and then changing the beliefs in the evening.

You may also find it useful to apply the same technique to your days: keep a notebook on your desk to write down any business blocks that you notice throughout the day. If you find yourself procrastinating on something that you know would help you to grow your business, like doing webinars or videos, then make a note of it. These are the symptoms that indicate business blocks at a deeper level.

Then, if you've already trained in a technique that helps you transform your beliefs at the subconscious level, you can use that in the evenings to release your blocks. If you prefer to work with someone else, like a PSYCH-K® facilitator or another type of practitioner or therapist, you've got valuable information to bring to your session with them. You'll know exactly which business blocks you're experiencing and exactly what you need to work on during your session. This method can help you get even more out of each session with your practitioner or therapist because you'll be able to work more quickly and easily.

For now, let's take a look at the fifteen categories of business blocks.

**On the podcast**

You can find the full list of podcast episodes here:
www.hollyworton.com/podcast

- 153 Holly Worton ~ 7 MORE Business Blocks That Hold Back Most Entrepreneurs & How to Release Them
- 149 Holly Worton ~ 7 Business Blocks That Hold Back Most Entrepreneurs & How to Release Them
- 135 Cathy Ballard ~ How to Find Your Flow And Bust Through Your Blocks in Business
- 90 How to Overcome Your Money Blocks, with Denise Duffield-Thomas
- 66 How to Heal Your Money Blocks, with Yiye Zhang

9

# HOW TO CHANGE AT THE DEEPER LEVELS

"If we could get your subconscious mind to agree with your conscious mind about being happy, that's when your positive thoughts work."

— Bruce Lipton

Affirmations don't work. At least, not as well as some people would lead you to believe. This is a divisive statement, and I know that many people don't feel the same as I do about affirmations. If I've just triggered a knee jerk reaction in you, please read on so you can understand my logic here. I think they're a good start: if you had never heard about doing mindset work at the deeper levels, then affirmations would be better than nothing. They get you focused on what you *do* want—rather than what you *don't* want—and eventually, after many repetitions, they'll sink into your subconscious.

You may be tempted to repeat some of these belief statements over and over as affirmations, and affirmations can indeed help change your beliefs at the *conscious* level.

But it takes ages of repetition to get them to get into your subconscious. And if your subconscious mind isn't on board, then it will be running its programs in the background and will end up effectively sabotaging your conscious efforts. Plus, by repeating affirmations, you won't be taking into account any energy blocks you may have.

Here's my problem with affirmations: they take so much time. You've got to repeat them every day. And you've got to *remember* to repeat them every day. Yes, they get you focused on your goals and intentions, but they're just not very useful in terms of the ratio of time-to-result. Thankfully, there's an easier way of doing it, and that's working at the subconscious and energetic levels. Hopefully, you've understood by now that it's faster and easier to work that way. I like easy, especially when so many of the other things I do in life are quite challenging.

Over the years, many of my clients have asked me to muscle test some of their favorite affirmations for them. They wanted to see if their subconscious mind believed them or not. Inevitably, they test weak, which means that their subconscious mind does not accept the affirmations that they've been dutifully repeating for weeks on end. People are always surprised when this happens, but I've seen it so many times with so many clients that it's led me to believe that affirmations are a complete waste of time. (Again, if they work for you, then keep at it—but if they *really* work for you, then why are you reading this book?)

Now, I know that "affirmations don't work" is a strong statement, because I do believe that they can be useful at the *conscious* level. But why waste your time repeating an affirmation over and over for hundreds—or thousands—of times, when you can change a belief at the deeper levels, more quickly and easily, in just a few minutes? Yes, you read that right. It's possible to completely reprogram your beliefs at the deeper levels in only a few minutes.

## Work alone or with someone else

You may choose to do the work alone, with yourself, if you've trained in a technique that works to change beliefs. You may also want to work with someone else. For me, the perfect solution is to work both with myself *and* with other professionals.

I do regular work with myself using Heart-centered Energy Work®, and I also work with other professionals using other techniques. I find this the most effective way to work. There are many things that I can see that need to be worked on, and I do the work on them. But there are other things that I find it difficult to see because I need a fresh, different perspective on them, and that's where another professional can come in and help me to pick apart the issue that I need to work on.

Another practitioner or facilitator can help me to see a new perspective on a situation, and they can also help me to dig deeper into an issue and push me to work on things that I may not have considered on my own. Again, each person needs to find their own best way of working on their business beliefs, but in my experience, I've gotten great results with this combination approach.

## Work at the deeper levels

I'm of the school of thought that only *you* know what's best for you (this should be clear by this point in the book). I recognize that there is no one technique or solution for everyone, and there's a whole range of other tools out there that work at the deeper levels. Find the best method for you:

- Heart-centered Energy Work®
- PSYCH-K®
- ThetaHealing®
- Emotional Freedom Techniques® (EFT or tapping)
- NLP (Neuro-Linguistic Programming)
- TAT (Tapas Acupressure Technique)
- Ask & Receive
- hypnotherapy
- ...or something else

Search online for the different options and speak with friends to see what's worked for them. But keep in mind that what's worked for someone else may or may not work for you. Sometimes your journey will involve trial and error until you find what's best for you. I tried so many things over the years before I found what worked best for me, and eventually, that evolved into me channeling my process, Heart-centered Energy Work®.

My guides once described HEW® as a spiritual process in an envelope of magic, whereas other techniques I've worked with have very much been a mental process. They were the right thing for me at that time, and as I've grown, I'm now working with something that I find even more effective—for me. Again, do what works for *you*.

**Subconscious + energy**

I clearly understand that the power of HEW® is that it works by simultaneously reprogramming beliefs at the subconscious level and releasing energy blocks by transforming the energy centers in our bodies. Working at these two deep levels at the same time, in the same process is what helps both my clients and me to get fast, long-lasting results. But again, you need to use the technique that gets you results, and that feels right for you.

**Take action today**

Have you heard of any of the methods and techniques that I mentioned above? What are some others that you're aware of that I haven't discussed? Have you tried any of them? Did you like them? Did they get you the results that you wanted? If you've never heard of any of these techniques, go online and read up on them. See which one (or ones) you're most drawn to, and give it a try.

For example, I recently read a book that discussed TRE® (Tension & Trauma Releasing Exercises) as a way of releasing trauma from where it's been stored in the body. My gut instantly said, "YES!" and I went online and found a provider in my area. In just over a week, I was at her home having my first session.

Go with what feels right or what catches your attention. There's a reason you're drawn to it.

# 10

# CATEGORIES OF BLOCKS

"The eye sees only what the mind is prepared to comprehend."

— Robertson Davies

I've divided up these business blocks into the same fifteen categories I presented in my book *Business Beliefs*; I consider these to be the essential facets of business mindset that I've regularly worked on with clients over the years. The categories include:

1. Action and Goals
2. Change and Growth
3. Clients and Boundaries
4. Confidence and Self-Trust
5. Creativity
6. Leadership and Outsourcing
7. Learning
8. Lifestyle
9. Marketing and Sales

10. Money
11. Personal Power
12. Strategy, Clarity and Vision
13. Success and Opportunities
14. Value and Self-Worth
15. Visibility

In the following chapters, I share examples from my work with clients as well as my own stories. I do this to help you uncover your blocks. Sometimes, reading someone else's story makes you realize you've been experiencing something similar.

You may find that you have more work to do in some areas, and you may find that you have very little work to do in other areas. In any case, it's worth going through each category and exploring the questions in each chapter. You may uncover blocks that you didn't even know you had.

I'm good at some things: for example, creativity and learning. Sometimes I'm good with action-taking and goal-setting. Sometimes I'm good with change and growth. I've struggled in the past with setting and upholding boundaries, but I've improved in that area. I've struggled throughout my life with self-confidence, self-trust, leadership, personal power, self-value, self-worth, and visibility. I've had to work hard to improve my marketing and sales practices, despite having over a decade of experience from my first company.

Some things I'm good at; others are a big challenge. I believe that it's essential for us to know our strengths as well as our weaknesses. Which of these fifteen areas of business blocks come naturally to you? Which ones are more difficult?

And as I've said multiple times, this is like peeling off the layers of the onion: there are some things that you won't be able to see in yourself today, but they'll become more apparent once you start doing the mindset work to release your blocks. If you want to make this process as efficient as possible, it's essential to be willing to dig deep and uncover the shadow stuff—including the things that make you very uncomfortable. But no matter how you do the work, things will get better. Even if you're only ready, willing, and able to work on the surface level blocks, you'll start to see results. As the quote at the beginning of this chapter says, you'll only be able to see the things today that you're ready to understand right now. With work, you'll be able to go deeper and deeper.

### Action and Goals

Action-taking is a vital part of owning and operating a business. Let's go beyond that: it's an integral part of life. Without taking action, we won't get anywhere. Yet many of us procrastinate on taking the actions we need to take to achieve our goals in business and life. We're blocked in the area of action-taking and goal-setting.

### Change and Growth

Being an entrepreneur means being able to embrace change and growth. When we're blocked in this area, we stay stuck and stagnant. We avoid innovation and development, and our business can quickly fail. Blocks in this area can be fatal to a business.

### Clients and Boundaries

Customers and clients are the backbones of every business. Without them, the company won't exist. When we have blocks in this area, we obstruct the flow of money into our business and prevent any success.

### Confidence and Self-Trust

When we lack self-confidence and self-trust, business feels painful. It seems impossible to achieve anything. We may feel inclined to give up before we even get started. Some people can fake it until they make it, but not everybody can do this. Others who have blocks in this area will stay stuck, paralyzed with fear.

### Creativity

Being an entrepreneur is being creative: you're creating a business that you hope will be successful. And you'll be creating new products and services to offer to your customers and clients. When you're blocked in this area, it makes it hard to create new things, making your business boring and stagnant.

### Leadership and Outsourcing

When you own a business, you're a leader, whether you like it or not. But do you have the belief in yourself to stand up and step into this leadership role? If not, your business will suffer. And if you can't effectively outsource tasks to employees or freelancers, you'll be overwhelmed and ineffective as a leader. It's important to release any blocks you may have in this area.

### Learning

Being an entrepreneur means learning new things... constantly. It requires staying on top of industry trends. If you have blocks in this area because you believe you're not a fast learner, or you're not good with technology (for example), then your business will suffer.

### Lifestyle

It's essential to create a business that fits into the lifestyle that you want. It makes no sense to leave a job you were unhappy with to build a company that makes you even more miserable. Your lifestyle is an integral part of your business, and if you have blocks about your ability to have the lifestyle that you want, then you'll end up with a company that you hate.

### Marketing and Sales

Marketing and sales are how you get your customers and clients, the backbone of your business. If you've got blocks in this area, you won't be able to generate the revenue you need to grow your business. If the situation is truly dire, you may end up with a costly hobby instead of a business. You wouldn't be the first.

### Money

Money: if it's not flowing into your business, then something's not right. Many people have such severe money blocks that it affects their ability to create and grow a business. That's why this is one of the essential categories of business blocks.

### Personal Power

Personal power is a feeling—a sense of being—made up of the layers of self-trust, self-love, self-acceptance, self-esteem, self-confidence, self-value, self-worth that we have within ourselves. It's a sense of groundedness. And if we have blocks in this area, it will make it very, very difficult to create a successful business. We need to trust ourselves, love ourselves, accept ourselves, value ourselves and have confidence in ourselves. This work is a big project that can take years to achieve, and the sooner we get started, the sooner we'll see results.

### Strategy, Clarity, and Vision

Running a successful business is all about having a clear vision (see chapter 7) and a plan to achieve it. Some people are so blocked that they don't know what they want for their business, much less understand how they're going to get there. So they take random actions, wandering around in circles. If you're blocked in this area, you may feel like you've been taking shots in the dark and not hitting anything—because you don't even know what you're aiming at.

### Success and Opportunities

Success means different things to different people. Having a successful business may be about making seven figures each year. It may mean bringing in just enough money but having the flexibility to have a rewarding family life. If we're blocked in this area—either because we're afraid of failure, or we're scared of success, or something else entirely—it's going to make it very, very difficult to build the business we want.

### Value and Self-Worth

When we don't value ourselves, we find it hard to succeed. We find it challenging to get clients, and when we do, we may undercharge and overdeliver. It's hard to run a business this way, and when we have self-worth blocks, this can often lead to a company never getting off the ground.

### Visibility

If people don't know who you are, then they can't hire you or buy your products. If you're the best-kept secret in your field, then you won't be bringing in business. Visibility blocks can cost you your success. If you're afraid of standing out in the crowd, then it's pretty much guaranteed that you're going to blend in—and that's not good for business.

11

# ACTION AND GOAL BLOCKS

"Any action is often better than no action, especially if you have been stuck in an unhappy situation for a long time. If it is a mistake, at least you learn something, in which case it's no longer a mistake. If you remain stuck, you learn nothing."

— Eckhart Tolle

I've organized the different categories of blocks in alphabetical order, in the same way that I organized them in my *Business Beliefs* book. But looking at our action and goal blocks is probably one of the most natural places to start because it's so easy to uncover them. Blocks in this area can also be symptoms of even deeper blocks that fall into other categories. The most significant sign of action and goal blocks is that you don't take the actions that you need to take to achieve your business goals. Have you been procrastinating lately? If so, then let's take a look at what's going on there.

I like to think of myself as an action taker, and I am...

sometimes. Yet I know I've struggled with taking action in the past. I remember working with my first big-name business coach a few years back: I would agree to take a particular action or work on a project, and then the thought of doing it would make me sick with fear. I would often procrastinate until the day before our next session when I'd finally do the work that I agreed to get done, because I couldn't bear to show up to the meeting and tell her that I hadn't done the work.

Yet when I'd write an email to someone asking to do a joint venture, or pitch myself to be a guest on someone else's podcast, or whatever the action was that I'd agreed to take, I would be doing it from the place of just wanting to get it done and get it over with. I wasn't doing it with the right intentions or the right energy. The emails would be awkward and apologetic, rather than clear and confident.

After getting my first book, *Business Beliefs*, ready for publication, I delayed its release by about three months because of "stuff" that came up. I absolutely could have released the book at any point during those three months, but I didn't get around to it. Now I understand that I was blocking myself because I was so scared to release my first book. I had placed so much importance on its release that I was terrified to put it out into the world. What would people think? What if I got a bad review? What if everyone hated it?

Since this first book, I've gone on to write a total of nine books and one workbook, not including the companion workbook to this title. I've received many excellent five-star reviews. And I've also received some pretty bad one-star ones. At first, these hurt. They felt like a punch in the gut. But the reviews are overwhelmingly positive, and I get emails all the time from people who have read my books and were helped by them, and that's what keeps me going: knowing that my books help people.

Imagine how many people you could help if you just got over your blocks and did the things you want to do in your business. Now, imagine how many people will miss out on being helped by you if you never take action to get over this stuff. What if they never find help anywhere else? This is a call to action for you to get over yourself and do the work you're here to do.

I also went through a period in my business where I just didn't set any goals for myself, which I now find hilarious because I'm such a goal setter. Every year, I plan out my goals and projects and map out the entire year to come. I love doing this. But back then, I had hit a point where I hadn't achieved my goals in so long that I didn't trust in my ability to accomplish any goals, so I didn't even bother setting them in the first place. Why set goals when you know you're only going to disappoint yourself? (Note—I don't recommend this strategy, but it was my line of thinking at the time.)

Another common thing—and that I've certainly done in the past—is to get caught up in busywork. There have been times when I've gotten so wrapped up in doing the small stuff (usually things that I could outsource to someone else) that I don't have time to do the necessary actions. I've kept my days filled doing busy work—like admin—rather than doing the important things that would grow my business. I spent so much time working *in* my business that I no longer had time to work *on* my business.

Have you ever had an addiction to social media or games? Those are other conventional ways of procrastinating. The worst part of this is that you can use social media as an excuse: you may go online to network and market your business and then end up watching cat videos or scrolling through Reddit for a half hour—or more. I know I've been there: I've gone through periods in my life where I spent far too much time on social media and games on my phone...to the point where I had to set limits on my phone to remind myself to stop what I was doing and get back to work.

So, as you can see, I'm a goal setter, and I'm an action taker...except when I'm not. When I allow my blocks to get in the way, I often cease goal-setting entirely, and I end up taking all the wrong actions. Not a good plan.

### Symptoms of blocks

Here's a more detailed explanation of signs that you may be struggling with blocks in the area of Action and Goals. Be sure to make a note of which ones you're currently experiencing in your business. If any of these trigger an understanding of different blocks that you're experiencing, do write those down, too. It's essential to get all of this out of your head and onto paper (or into a computer file), where you can then work with them.

Do any of these resonate with you?

- You rarely achieve your business goals. Or maybe it's even worse than that: you don't even bother to set any goals in the first place. You know you *should*, but it just never seems to happen.
- Your to-do list never gets completed. It keeps growing by the days and weeks with all the actions that you know will help you to grow your business, but you never actually get around to doing them. Every time you think of that to-

do list, you get an anxious feeling in your gut. You'll never get through it all!
- You get the quickest and easiest tasks done first, rather than choosing your top three most important actions that will move your business forward. Those big actions look too daunting, and it's just easier to get the little things done first, even when they're so simple that you could easily outsource them to a virtual assistant.
- You suffer from inconsistency. You may start a task, but you can't keep the momentum going, and it never gets done. Or you write one blog post, but then it takes you six weeks to sit down and do the next one. Maybe you manage to batch a month's worth of videos in one afternoon, but then you don't do another video for the next six months (I know I've done this one before).
- You struggle to create a structure around what you do, so you haven't been able to create the signature system that your business coach has been at you to put together.

**Common fears**

Here are some common fears relating to action-taking and goal-setting:

- Fear of taking the wrong actions
- Fear of making decisions
- Fear of doing a lot of work and still failing
- Fear of not achieving goals
- Fear of achieving a goal and realizing it's not what we really wanted

**Discover your blocks**

Here are a few questions to help you get clear on your business blocks:

- Let's look at your business goals. Have you set clear goals that are specific and measurable? Are they written down where you can review them regularly?
- Do you review your goals periodically?
- Do you have a clear plan to achieve these goals? If not, what's stopping you? What are you afraid of?
- What beliefs do you hold that are preventing you from setting clear goals and creating a plan to achieve them?
- One of the best ways to uncover blocks in this area is to ask yourself the following question: what do you procrastinate on? Often the things we most procrastinate on are the things that take us out of our comfort zone. Interestingly, these are also actions that will lead us to more significant results in our business. So...what are you procrastinating on? And why?
- What's stopping you from prioritizing your to-do list and getting started?
- And what's stopping you from choosing three of the most critical tasks on your to-do list each day and getting those done first?
- What's stopping you from selecting ten of the little things on your list and outsourcing them to a virtual assistant? For this exercise, don't use money as a reason: assume you've got the funds

to hire a VA and then ask yourself the question: why haven't you hired one yet?

- Do you struggle to delegate tasks to someone else because you're afraid they won't get completed to your standards?
- Are you a perfectionist? Is that why things aren't getting done on your list?
- Do you struggle to live by the motto "good enough is better than perfect"?
- Why do you think you find it so challenging to create content regularly, like blog posts, email newsletters, or podcast episodes (assuming this is part of your business strategy)?
- What's holding you back from batching and releasing content consistently?
- What might make it easier for you?
- Are you afraid of taking up space on people's Facebook timelines? Do you worry about "bothering" people with your content?
- What's holding you back from creating a structured signature system or online program (again, assuming this is part of your business strategy)? Is this something you want to do, or do you think you should do it because "everyone else is"?
- Do you believe that there's no natural system for what you do?
- Are you afraid of standing out and being judged for creating your system?

**Examples of blocks**

Sometimes it can be hard to identify our blocks, especially if we're getting started digging them up. Here are some examples that might help you to identify your business blocks in the area of Action and Goals:

- You're afraid of failure, and if you don't take action toward your goals, then you have the perfect excuse to fail in your business. You see, it's not that you're not good at what you do, it's just that you never got around to taking the action you needed to take to make your business work. Back to the day job, because that's safely inside your comfort zone.
- You're afraid of success, and if you don't take action toward your goals, then you have the perfect excuse not to succeed in your business. This block is more common than you may think. Success puts us out there in a big way, and often we don't feel ready for it. That means that it's easier to play small and stay stuck in our comfort zone. (If this is the case, refer to the chapter on Visibility Blocks, which will help you dig even deeper into this area. You'll find that some of these blocks are symptoms of even deeper blocks, so I'll be cross-referencing the different categories of blocks throughout the book.)
- You're terrified of putting yourself out there in a more significant way and being visible online with your business. That's why you haven't started blogging, or creating videos for your YouTube channel, or looking for speaking opportunities. (If this is the case, refer to the chapter on Visibility Blocks, which will help you dig even deeper into this area.)

**On the podcast**

You can find the full list of podcast episodes here: www.hollyworton.com/podcast

- 181 Jo + Holly ~ Is Mindset Important in Business, or Is It Just an Excuse to Avoid Action?
- 166 Holly Worton ~ How to Drop the Hustle and Start Taking Easy Inspired Action Instead

## 12

# CHANGE AND GROWTH BLOCKS

"Change will not come if we wait for some other person or some other time. We are the ones we've been waiting for. We are the change that we seek."

— Barack Obama

Fear of change is a huge issue for many entrepreneurs. You'd think that we'd be invincible, wouldn't you? We're willing to quit our job, which offers a steady paycheck, and venture into the world of entrepreneurial inconsistency, where it can be feast or famine for the first few months—or longer!—of business. This takes strength, it takes courage, and it takes resilience.

But deep down, sometimes we actually fear change and growth. It takes us out of our comfort zone into something new and exciting...and scary. It's a journey into the unknown. And as we've discussed, your subconscious will want to keep you safe inside the known region of your comfort zone.

I've been through many iterations of my business over

the years. I started out helping businesses with their social media marketing, then I moved into helping entrepreneurs with their business mindset. And I had many different versions of each of those businesses. I changed my business niche many, many times. Each time, I knew in my gut that it was the right thing to do, yet I always worried what people would think of me, changing my mind yet again. I worried they would think I was flaky and unprofessional, and yet if I hadn't allowed myself to pivot all those times, and change my path, I wouldn't have ended up where I am today, which is a much more aligned place for me. Perhaps I would have ended up here anyway, but I imagine it would have taken me much, much longer.

I know that when I rebranded my business and put more of *me* into the look and feel of everything, I was simultaneously excited *and* sick to my stomach. What would people think? It was so much easier to hide behind the safety of my old Ready to Bloom brand, but I knew the time had come to grow into a new brand that was more about *me*. I had done the mindset work that allowed this to happen, but I still felt scared, and eventually I needed to do even more work to release the fears. It all made me feel so exposed and visible, which is of course what you want in a business, but it certainly wasn't easy.

In late 2018, I decided to let go of my business mindset services to focus on my writing. Deep in my gut, I knew this was the right decision for me, but it was terrifying all the same. I was choosing to let go of an important part of my identity—as a self-proclaimed "business mindset alchemist"—and step into the new identity of "author". By this point, I had already written eight books, so I already was an established author, but it was still terrifying. The change in identity wasn't easy.

And speaking of identity—when I left my first company

that I had run for ten years, that was a very difficult change in my life. I knew it was the right decision for me, but so much of my identity was wrapped up in that company, that I no longer had any idea who I was. It was a very, very difficult decision to make, and I really struggled with getting to know myself and my new identity in the months afterward.

**Symptoms of blocks**

Here's a more detailed explanation of symptoms that you may be struggling with blocks in the area of Change and Growth. Be sure to make note of which ones you're currently experiencing in your business.

Do any of these resonate with you?

- Your business is exactly the same now as it was six months ago. Same income (or lack of), same frustrations. Nothing new.
- You're starting to feel like you've grown out of your current business, and that it's time for a change. Maybe a re-brand, or even changing your business niche. But you've done nothing about it.
- You've been running your business for some time, alongside a full time or part time job. Your business has been growing, and your job has now become a hindrance rather than a support. It's time to quit your job, but you just can't bear to do it.
- Something's not feeling quite right with your business mentor or coach, and you're not getting the same results as you used to from your sessions with her. You suspect it might be time to find a new mentor or coach, but how can you

not renew your subscription to her program or package?

- You're dying to hire a virtual assistant and free up some extra time during your week, but you keep putting it off.

### Common fears

Here are some common fears relating to change and growth:

- Fear of change
- Fear of not being able to change and staying the same forever
- Fear of the unknown
- Fear of outgrowing a group of business friends
- Fear of not being able to handle the things that come with change

### Discover your blocks

Here are a few questions to help you get clear on your business blocks:

- Why do you think your business is exactly the same today as it was six months ago (assuming this is the case)? Why is your income still the same?
- Why are you still frustrated with the same things?
- What's stopping you from changing things up and bringing in more clients?
- Why do you think you haven't you gotten help

with the things that frustrate you and make you feel stuck in your business?

- What's holding you back from re-branding your business or even changing your niche? Is it because everyone knows you as the [insert your business niche here] expert?
- Do you believe that if you change your brand or your niche, people will think you're unprofessional? Are you afraid of looking like you're "too big for your britches"? That people might judge you for expanding into a new look for your business?
- If you're still employed, why haven't you quit your job yet, assuming it's the right moment to dedicate yourself full time to your business? Is it because you're afraid to take the leap of faith in your business and let go of the steady pay check? Is it because you don't believe, deep down, that you have what it takes to run a successful business?
- Are you afraid that your recent success is all a fluke, and it's all going to go downhill sometime soon?
- Why haven't you made plans to find another business coach or mentor? Is it because you're afraid that your new coach night not be as good as this one is? Are you afraid of hurting your current mentor's feelings by making a change?
- What's stopping you from hiring a virtual assistant? Is it because you're wondering how you can possibly outsource these tasks to someone else?
- Are you stressing that they won't get done exactly how you do them?

- Are you worried that your VA will do things differently (meaning: not as good as you)? Are you thinking that it's better to keep doing these tasks yourself...that way you have full control over how things get done?

**Examples of blocks**

Sometimes it can be hard to identify our blocks, especially if we're just getting started digging them up. Here are some examples that might help you to identify your business blocks in the area of Change and Growth:

- You believe it's hard to change, and that change takes time. You don't expect to see any change or growth in your business anytime soon. Maybe in a year or two. After all, doesn't it take at least three years to turn a profit in your business? You seem to remember having read that somewhere. It must be true.
- Change is stressful. That's just how it is. Always. And you've got enough stress in your life, so why add more? Better to just keep things the way they are.
- Change is scary. Who knows what's coming next? It's safe here inside your comfort zone. And things are much, much easier here. At least you know what's going on here.

**On the podcast**

You can find the full list of podcast episodes here: www.hollyworton.com/podcast

- 333 Holly Worton ~ Do You Have a Fixed Mindset or a Growth Mindset?
- 332 Joanna Hennon + Holly ~ How to Step Into a New Identity Even When You're Not Sure What It Looks Like
- 273 Holly Worton ~ What Change Actually Looks Like
- 251 Holly Worton ~ How to Step Into a New Business Identity
- 196 Marianne Cantwell ~ How to Make Big Changes in Your Business in an Unconventional Way
- 64 How to Tame Your Business Beast and Automate Your Growth, with Tina Forsyth

# 13

# CLIENT AND BOUNDARY BLOCKS

"When you're the most successful person in your family, in your neighborhood, and in your town, everybody thinks you're the First National Bank, and you have to figure out for yourself where those boundaries are."

— Oprah Winfrey

There are so many things that can come up for us around clients. If we're starting out, we may believe we have to take on every single person that approaches us, because if we turn anyone down, that will make it harder to get more clients in the future. We may struggle to set boundaries with clients, believing we have to work all hours of the day or night, especially if we have an online business where we work with people in different time zones.

Boundaries have been a big learning point for me in this lifetime—within my business and in my personal life. I've had to do a lot of mindset work around my boundaries with clients. You may have heard me tell the story on my podcast of a VIP day client who was three hours late for her six-hour session. I also talk about that in my *Business Beliefs* book. Yes, she paid me extra when we made up the time the following day, and yes, I was able to get some work done while I waited, but this is something that I just wouldn't put up with these days. I've done the mindset work so that I can set and uphold clear boundaries with clients. I honestly cringe when I think of some of the things I put up with in my early days.

On the other side of things—from the client perspective, I once booked a 60-minute session with a therapist who asked me to block off 90 minutes in my calendar because sometimes she went overtime. That 60-minute session ended up turning into a two and a half-hour session! While I was grateful for the extra time she spent with me—we got lots of work done!—I was exhausted from everything that we did. We were working so long that we had to take a bathroom break halfway through! If I had known in advance that we'd be working for so long, I would have been more prepared.

This session is a perfect example of a therapist not setting clear boundaries for herself when working with clients: essentially, she gave me over twice the time that I paid for (two and a half times, if you want to get specific). I understand that sometimes we need to go overtime by five minutes or so, but this was ridiculous. I know a lot of new coaches and therapists struggle with bringing a session to a close, especially when they're first starting.

I once had a discovery call with a potential client who lived in the town where I live. By this point, I was only offering online sessions and not face-to-face sessions. She was very disappointed that we couldn't meet up for the session in person, especially considering that we were in the same town. But I had quit doing sessions at the local therapy room, and I stuck to my boundaries. She ended up not working with me, and I'm not sure if it was for that reason or something else, but I no longer enjoyed holding face-to-face sessions, and I wasn't going to budge. A couple of years prior, I probably would have gone out of my way to accommodate her.

And in terms of setting clear boundaries for your working hours, I guarantee that when people want to work with you, they'll make it happen—even if you've got wildly different time zones. When I was diagnosed with Aspergers Syndrome in 2015, I knew I wanted to work with a particular professional—Tania Marshall—who specialized in women with Aspergers and who lived in Australia. The times she had available for me to work with her were either early in the morning or late at night—either 6 to 9 am or 11 pm to 1 am. She knew that I was in the UK, and she didn't offer me any other options, which was okay with me. I didn't ask her if she had any additional hours available because I respected her schedule. I happily chose the nighttime session, and I was very grateful to be able to work with her. If people want you, they'll accept the hours you offer them—don't feel the need to work ridiculous hours if you don't want to.

## Symptoms of blocks

Here's a more detailed explanation of symptoms that you may be struggling with blocks in the area of Clients. Be sure to make a note of which ones you're currently experiencing in your business.

Do any of these resonate with you?

- It's either feast or famine in your business. You

seem to get an influx of clients, and then nothing for weeks on end.
- You're terrible at setting boundaries with clients. You run overtime on your sessions, and you agree to see clients outside of your regular working hours to accommodate their needs: early in the morning, late in the evening, even on weekends.
- You occasionally have clients that are a joy to work with. Unfortunately, most of them are a complete pain. They don't do the work, so they end up not getting the results they want, which means these clients are not happy with the investment they've made with you.
- Lots of people seem to be interested in what you do, but no one seems to have the money to invest in your products and services.
- You haven't even bothered putting up a Testimonials page on your website because you don't have any testimonials to share.

**Common fears**

Here are some common fears relating to clients and boundaries:

- Fear that you'll never have enough clients
- Fear that clients will never pay what you want to earn
- Fear that clients will hate the way you work
- Fear that clients will be upset when you cancel a session because they were late
- Fear of bad reviews online

### Discover your blocks

Here are a few questions to help you get clear on your business blocks:

- What's stopping you from having a steady stream of clients? Are you charging by the hour for individual sessions, rather than creating packages that your ideal clients would find attractive?
- Are you afraid of asking clients for the more substantial sum of money that a package would cost because it just seems cheaper and more accessible for them to work with you by the hour?
- Why is it that you think you need to be available 24 hours a day, seven days a week for your clients? Do you believe that if you're not always there for them, then they'll work with someone else?
- Are you afraid that if you don't go overtime with your sessions, that your clients won't feel like they've had great value from your work together?
- Do you believe that "nice coaches/therapists/whatever" give their clients extra time for free?
- Why do you think you struggle to attract great clients?
- Are you clear on who your ideal clients are, and why you love them so much?
- Do you find it hard to say no to clients who express interest in working with you?
- Is it difficult to refer potential clients to someone

else if they don't feel like a good fit? Do you believe you have to take on every client that comes your way?
- Are you so desperate for the money that you feel like you have to take every client who approaches you?
- Why do you think you're attracting people who like what you do but aren't willing to invest?
- Could you change the way you market your business and try to attract clients who are willing to pay your fees?
- Do you truly understand the value of the work that you do with clients, or do you secretly believe that your work isn't good enough? (If this is the case, refer to the chapter on Value and Self-Worth Blocks, which will help you dig even deeper into this area.)
- What's stopping you from getting testimonials from all of your clients?
- Are you afraid that they'll say no?
- Are you worried they'll tell you they didn't get any results from the work that they did with you, and that it was a waste of money?
- Are you worried that you'll annoy them by asking for a testimonial?

### Examples of blocks

Sometimes it can be hard to identify our blocks, especially if we're getting started digging them up. Here are some examples that might help you to identify your business blocks in the area of Clients:

- It's hard to get a steady stream of clients. There's

no real way to guarantee a steady income when you're self-employed because there are too many factors involved.
- If I don't agree to see clients on evenings and weekends, I'll never find enough clients to keep my business going. People need me to be flexible.
- Working only with my ideal clients is a luxury that I can't afford at this point in my business, so I've got to say yes to working with everyone who approaches me.

**On the podcast**

You can find the full list of podcast episodes here: www.hollyworton.com/podcast

- 184 Rebecca Miller ~ How to Use Case Studies to Get Great Publicity & Reach Your Ideal Clients
- 173 Jo & Holly ~ Should You Guarantee Results For Your Clients
- 154 Arabelle Yee ~ How to Create Unique Packages Personalized for Each Client
- 143 RM Harrison ~ How to Clone Your Favorite Client
- 121 Jo Casey ~ How to Get Coaching Clients Without the Hustle
- 106 Nicci Bonfanti ~ How to Serve Your Clients Through Selling
- 82 How to Create a High End Offer Your Clients Will Buy, with Julia Bernard-Thompson
- 38 How to Get More Clients Saying Yes, with Catherine Watkin

## 14

## CONFIDENCE AND SELF-TRUST BLOCKS

"One important key to success is self-confidence. An important key to self-confidence is preparation."

— Arthur Ashe

This area is a significant source of blocks for many entrepreneurs. We may lack the confidence and trust in ourselves that we can create a successful business on our terms. This can especially be an issue if we don't have any past business experience and have always had a job with a steady paycheck.

Confidence has always been a big issue for me. I was never self-confident as a child or as a teenager. As an adult, I lacked confidence in a big way, in part a result of working with a business partner for years who consistently put down the quality of my work. It's taken *years* of mindset work to build up my confidence in my skills and abilities to help my clients. I've had to reprogram many, many limiting beliefs and blocks that were holding me back.

When I started my first coaching business, I thought it would be easy. At that point, I had ten years of business and marketing experience under my belt, but it wasn't easy at all. In theory, I knew everything I needed to know to run a business, but what I didn't have was the confidence—the confidence in myself and my abilities as a coach. That took time—and a lot of mindset work.

I also have lots of issues around having the confidence to ask for help. I'm always happy to review a friend's book or help a friend with her new online program by posting about it on social media. But when it comes to asking others to do the same for me? That's tough. I've done lots of work on it being safe and appropriate to ask others for help, and as a result, it's much easier for me to ask someone for a review on Amazon when they send me an email praising my book.

Self-trust has also been a big issue for me. There was much gaslighting in my relationship with my first business partner. Gaslighting is when someone manipulates someone else into doubting their reality, and even their sanity. There was a time when I didn't trust myself, and I didn't trust my decisions—I was so confused that I didn't know up from down, left from right. This trauma took *years* of mindset work to unravel, and I'm finally at the point where I can trust myself and my intuition. One of my business mindset books is titled *Business Intuition* because I think it's such an essential aspect of our business mindset.

**Symptoms of blocks**

Here's a more detailed explanation of symptoms that you may be struggling with blocks in the area of Confidence and Self-Trust. Be sure to make a note of which ones you're currently experiencing in your business. Do any of these resonate with you?

- You've been working with clients for a while, but you're not confident that you know enough or have enough experience to help them.
- You've been in business for some time now, but you're just not sure you're going to make it.
- You second-guess yourself every time you have to make a business decision, no matter how big or small. How can you possibly know what the right thing to do is?
- You're afraid of being overconfident and coming across as a snob.
- Your business coach has asked you to approach at least five people before your next session that you can do a joint venture with, but you're terrified of reaching out to people.

**Common fears**

Here are some common fears relating to confidence and self-trust:

- Fear of not being able to run a business
- Fear of being seen as a fraud
- Fear that you won't be able to hold space properly with a client
- Fear of disappointing clients
- Fear that you'll be terrible in a presentation

**Discover your blocks**

Here are a few questions to help you get clear on your business blocks:

- What's affecting your confidence in the work that you do?
- Have you received negative feedback from many clients, or are you merely imagining that they're unhappy?
- What's stopping you from asking all clients for feedback, so you can learn how they truly feel about their work with you?
- Are you afraid you'll get your feelings hurt? Feel rejected or criticized?
- What's the root cause of your lack of faith that you can create a successful business?
- Do you have friends and family members telling you that you can't do it?
- Have you "failed" in business in the past?
- Have you seen others "fail" in business, and you're afraid you'll do the same?
- Have you made "bad" business decisions in the past that didn't work out for you?
- Have you had so many "failed" businesses that you don't have faith in your ability to make it work this time?
- What's stopping you from feeling confident in your business decisions?
- What's leading to your fear of being overconfident?
- Are you worried that your family will talk about you behind your back and you'll lose all your friends?

- What's going on there for you?
- What's the worst that could happen if people thought you were a snob?
- What's stopping you from approaching those joint venture partners? Are you afraid they'll say no? That they won't want to be associated with you? That they'll say that it's not a good fit? Is it fear of rejection?
- What's the worst that could happen if they said no?

**Examples of blocks**

Sometimes it can be hard to identify our blocks, especially if we're getting started digging them up. Here are some examples that might help you to identify your business blocks in the area of Confidence and Self-Trust:

- I've made so many mistakes in the past that I don't trust myself to make sound business decisions.
- My business has been struggling for so long that maybe I'm just not good at business. I'd better go back to my old job if I can still get it. I'm a business failure.
- My self-confidence is crap, and it always has been. I can't manage to make things work for myself.

**On the podcast**

You can find the full list of podcast episodes here: www.hollyworton.com/podcast

- 285 Holly Worton ~ How to Trust in Yourself & Trust That Everything is Working Out
- 243 Holly Worton ~ How to Trust Yourself in Business
- 213 Holly Worton ~ How to Face the Shadow Side of Visibility With Confidence
- 78 How to Get Confidence & Crush Self-Doubt, with Jenn Scalia

# 15

# CREATIVITY BLOCKS

"Don't think. Thinking is the enemy of creativity. It's self-conscious, and anything self-conscious is lousy. You can't try to do things. You simply must do things."

— Ray Bradbury

As I mentioned earlier, I haven't really struggled with creative blocks. There have been times when I've been able to be more creative than others, but it's not been a big issue for me personally.

However, I've worked with many clients who struggle to create content for their blog, their YouTube channel, or their social media profiles. They just don't consider themselves to be naturally creative people. Sometimes, creativity blocks can be intertwined with other types of blocks.

If we have blocks around value and self-worth, then we may not feel worthy enough to tell our story in a blog post or a video. If we have blocks around our successes not being big enough, then we may hesitate to share about our smaller successes. If we lack confidence and have low self-esteem, we may write a blog post, but not share it online.

### Symptoms of blocks

Here's a more detailed explanation of symptoms that you may be struggling with blocks in the area of Creativity. Be sure to make a note of which ones you're currently experiencing in your business.

Do any of these resonate with you?

- You love the idea of creating videos but haven't done anything about it.
- You know you "should" blog regularly, but you have no inspiration to sit down and write something.
- You're stuck with the copywriting for your new website because you can't focus. And your web developer won't be able to get anything done until you send her the copy.
- You cringe at the thought of creating graphics for your blog posts and social media. People have recommended some good online tools to use, but you just haven't done anything about it.
- You want to write a book/create videos/get speaking engagements, but you don't even bother starting the process because you know it's not for you.

### Common fears

Here are some common fears relating to creativity:

- Fear that no one cares what you have to say

- Fear of saying the wrong thing
- Fear of negative comments or reviews online
- Fear that people will think you're not original
- Fear that people will mock your story

**Discover your blocks**

Here are a few questions to help you get clear on your business blocks:

- What's stopping you from creating videos? Is it fear of technology? Is it that you don't know how to film and edit videos? Or that you don't know what equipment you need to get?
- Are you afraid of critical comments on YouTube?
- Are you afraid of sharing your videos on Facebook and taking up space on people's timelines?
- Are you afraid of being more visible online? (If this is the case, refer to the chapter on Visibility Blocks, which will help you dig even deeper into this area.)
- First of all, who says you "should" blog regularly? Who says you should blog at all? Do you want to blog? Do you even like writing?
- Or is it that you want to blog, but you believe you're not a good writer?
- Are you afraid of negative comments on your blog posts?
- Are you afraid of being more visible online? (If this is the case, refer to the chapter on Visibility Blocks, which will help you dig even deeper into this area.)

- What's stopping you from getting the copy written for your new website?
- Are you struggling to express who you are and what you do clearly?
- Are you clear about who your ideal clients are and whom you're writing for?
- Are you afraid to shine your light and stand out with your website copy?
- Are you afraid to look overconfident or cocky about what you do?
- Or do you feel, deep down, that you aren't that good at what you do, and you don't want to make a big deal out of it in your copy? (If this is the case, refer to the chapter on Confidence and Self- Trust Blocks, which will help you dig even deeper into this area.)
- What's going on with your procrastination on creating graphics for your blog posts and social media?
- Are you afraid you won't be able to create nice looking graphics, yet at the same time don't want to hire someone else to do it?
- Do you have issues around using technology?
- Are you concerned about overwhelming people with your graphics on their Facebook timelines?
- Are you afraid of being more visible online? (If this is the case, refer to the chapter on Visibility Blocks, which will help you dig even deeper into this area.)
- What's stopping you from getting creative in your business and writing a book, creating videos, or getting speaking engagements? Are you afraid that no one wants to hear what you

have to say? Are you worried that you won't be good at it?

**Examples of blocks**

Sometimes it can be hard to identify our blocks, especially if we're just getting started digging them up. Here are some examples that might help you to identify your business blocks in the area of Creativity:

- I'm just not a creative person. Writing a book, creating videos, or getting speaking engagements is for other people to do. I don't have what it takes.
- Writing/speaking/doing videos is hard. I don't have the experience as a writer/speaker/filmmaker, so I won't be able to do these things in my business.
- I lack the inspiration to be creative. Other people have such good ideas, but I can never think of anything.

**On the podcast**

You can find the full list of podcast episodes here: www.hollyworton.com/podcast

- 291 Holly Worton ~ How to Open Up & Be Vulnerable in Your Creative Ventures
- 249 Holly Worton ~ How to Help Your Business Blossom in Creative New Ways
- 83 How to Follow Your Creative Intuition, with Flora Bowley

16

# LEADERSHIP AND OUTSOURCING BLOCKS

"A genuine leader is not a searcher for consensus but a molder of consensus."

— Dr. Martin Luther King, Jr.

Leadership and outsourcing can be challenging areas for new business owners, especially for those who haven't had leadership or management roles in the past. It can take time to learn how to effectively lead a team of people or even delegate jobs to a single virtual assistant. Effectively outsourcing tasks to a VA or a team requires a skill set that has little to do with being able to do the tasks yourself.

These are the practical sides of leadership and outsourcing, and these realities can bring with them many blocks and limiting beliefs around our ability to be an effective leader and manager. We may even have made bad hiring decisions or have been ineffective managers in the past. Or we may have blocks around being a good leader and manager because of terrible managers we've experienced in the workplace.

I'm the first to admit that I was a terrible manager in my first company. I had no prior management experience, and I had no one to teach me how to do it well. My business partner was an awful manager, despite his opinion to the contrary. The management books I read were very corporate, and I couldn't figure out how to adapt their content to our smaller company of just 150 employees. My business partner, as I said, was also a bad manager, but in a different way—he was overbearing, controlling, and often micromanaged people. I found myself overcompensating by trying to be the "nice owner," which, as you might imagine, doesn't work very well. The "good cop, bad cop" game doesn't make for a good management team. I've had to do lots of work to undo the blocks that I created as a result of the very challenging ten years I spent running that business.

As a result of this first business experience, I had many blocks around leadership. Yes, I had been a leader in my first company, but it was so hard for me to see it. I didn't see myself as a leader, because my business partner had always undermined me and steamrolled over my values and preferences. It was like I was a leader in the shadows if that's even possible. I certainly was overpowered by his narcissistic personality, which outshined everyone else—or, instead, cast a dark shadow on everyone else.

And so it wasn't easy for me to recognize the times when I did step up as a leader: organizing PSYCH-K® practice days in London for other facilitators, starting the kind of podcast I wanted to listen to but couldn't find, and stepping up as a leader in the field of business mindset by writing these books. It was hard for me to see because I was blocked—I couldn't see myself as a leader.

Outsourcing wasn't as much of a problem for me—I had once owned and operated a company with 150 employees. I knew how to manage people (badly), and I knew how to hire people and delegate tasks. When I started my podcast in 2013, I knew from the start that I didn't want to learn how to edit the audio files myself, so I hired someone from the very beginning. But I've seen many entrepreneurs over the years struggle to relinquish the power of doing everything themselves and outsource tasks and projects to other people.

Often we think that other people won't do the work as well as we will. But ask yourself—is this true? I do not doubt that my podcast editor does a better job than I would. My bookkeeper and accountant do a better job than I would. My book cover designers do a better job than I would.

The list is endless. I cannot specialize in all the aspects of the work that I do, and I need to hire professionals who *do* specialize in those things. Yes, I can edit and proofread my books, but I also need to hire someone else to do the final edit and proofing.

### Symptoms of blocks

Here's a more detailed explanation of symptoms that you may be struggling with blocks in the area of Leadership and Outsourcing. Be sure to make a note of which ones you're currently experiencing in your business.

Do any of these resonate with you?

- Your business has been growing, and you're overwhelmed with things to do. Your business coach has suggested you hire a virtual assistant and get some help, but you've been putting it off.

- You're still playing small in your business, and you don't feel like a leader. Yes, you have paying clients, and they're happy with your work, but certainly, no one would consider you to be an expert in your field.
- To get things right, you *know* that you need to do them yourself. Other people manage to get everything done, so why can't you? You resist hiring a VA to do admin work, a bookkeeper to take care of your accounts, or a housekeeper to clean your home. You can do it all yourself.
- You're actively avoiding hiring staff for your business. Your best business friend has made lousy hire after lousy hire, wasting thousands, and getting deeper in debt. You've never actually hired people before, so you're probably destined to the same fate.
- You're good at what you do, and your clients are happy, but no one would ever consider you to be an inspiring leader in your field. At least, you don't feel that way.

### Common fears

Here are some common fears relating to leadership and outsourcing:

- Fear of being perceived as "too big for your britches"
- Fear of being seen as bossy
- Fear that people won't be on board with your ideas

- Fear that people won't like you if you stand up for your ideas and beliefs
- Fear that other people won't do the work as well as you can

**Discover your blocks**

Here are a few questions to help you get clear on your business blocks:

- If you're feeling overwhelmed with your to-do list, what's stopping you from hiring a VA and getting help?
- Are you concerned about hiring the right person?
- Are you afraid it will be a waste of money because the person will be irresponsible?
- Are you worried they'll make mistakes, and it will reflect poorly on your business reputation?
- What are you afraid of?
- Why do you think it is that people don't consider you to be an expert in your field?
- Are people just not aware that you exist?
- Are you avoiding putting yourself out there in a more significant way because you're scared of stepping up as a leader in your field?
- Are you afraid of being more visible?
- What's going on with this?
- Do you believe that other people won't be able to complete simple tasks as well as you?
- Do you honestly think that there's no one better than you to do your bookkeeping or housecleaning?

- What's stopping you from hiring someone to help you?
- Are you a perfectionist?
- What makes it difficult for you to hire the right person and trust that they'll do a great job under your supervision?
- Are you afraid you'll lose your Superwoman badge of honor if you start outsourcing to others?
- Do you honestly believe that just because other people make bad hiring decisions, that you will too?
- What's stopping you from hiring staff for your business?
- Are you afraid of managing people?
- Do you struggle to be the boss because you try to make people like you?
- Do you find it difficult to put boundaries in place between you and your staff?
- Have you been a not-so-great manager in the past?
- What's stopping you from seeing yourself as an inspiring leader in your field?
- Why do you struggle to see yourself as an inspiring example to your clients, and even to other entrepreneurs?
- Does the thought of being an inspiration to others scare you?
- How would you feel if someone told you that they found you to be inspiring?
- What comes up for you here?

### Examples of blocks

Sometimes it can be hard to identify our blocks, especially if we're just getting started digging them up. Here are some examples that might help you to identify your business blocks in the area of Leadership and Outsourcing:

- Leadership is hard for women. We have to pretend to be like men to be effective leaders.
- I'm not a leader. I lack what it takes. I've always been a follower, and that's what I'm meant to be. I can't change that. You're just born one way or the other.
- I could never outsource tasks to a VA. It's impossible to trust someone else to do things right. I'd waste more time supervising them than I would doing the things myself.

### On the podcast

You can find the full list of podcast episodes here: www.hollyworton.com/podcast

- 247 Holly Worton ~ What, When, Why, and How to Outsource

## 17

# LEARNING BLOCKS

"Every defeat, every heartbreak, every loss, contains its own seed, its own lesson on how to improve your performance next time."

— Malcolm X

I've worked with many women who have blocks around learning. Sometimes they're scared of technology and believe they'll never master the basics that they need to run their business. Other times they attend vital training for the technique they use in their business and struggle to absorb the information for one reason or another. Often, it has to do with blocks we've picked up at a younger age: things we've heard from our family, teachers, or peers.

This area is one that I'm not aware of struggling with. I mention this because I don't want you to feel like you have to have blocks in each of these fifteen categories of blocks. As I said before, I have Aspergers Syndrome, and my brain is naturally wired to be good at learning stuff on my own (my autism gives me plenty of challenges, but learning is not usually one of them). Everything I've learned about marketing and business in the twenty-plus years since I started my first company in 1999, I learned on my own. When I had to do something for the first time, I would go straight to the internet and search for how to do it. And then I'd do it.

But lots of people don't have the confidence and the belief that learning is easy for them. If you've ever had a traumatic experience with a teacher mocking you in class (yes, I've heard this story more than once) or if you've ever made a very public mistake during a school presentation, you've probably formed a series of blocks as a result of those experiences. If this is the case, then you might struggle to learn new material or to retain it. You may procrastinate trying new things in business because you're afraid of making a mistake. You may even think you're not cut out for being a business owner because of all the things you'll have to learn.

### Symptoms of blocks

Here's a more detailed explanation of symptoms that you may be struggling with blocks in the area of Learning. Be sure to make a note of which ones you're currently experiencing in your business.

Do any of these resonate with you?

- You resist setting up profiles on social media for your business. There are many different social networks out there, and you can't wrap your head around any of them. You cringe at the thought of getting started.
- You go to workshops and trainings and struggle

to absorb the information. You walk away from the course feeling like it was a total waste of time because you didn't learn much at all. The course content is all just muddled in your brain.
- You learn new things in workshops, but you struggle to retain the information and put it into practice. It was all clear during the workshop, and you were very excited about implementing what you learned, but it all faded away when the workshop was over.
- When you look at successful online entrepreneurs, you're so overcome by envy that you don't let yourself open yourself up to be inspired by what they do. You feel angry and bitter because you'll never be like them.
- You resist working with a business mentor. Everyone else seems to have a coach or a mentor, but you know it's just not for you.

### Common fears

Here are some common fears relating to learning:

- Fear of being too slow to learn all the things an entrepreneur needs to learn
- Fear of technology
- Fear of doing things in a new way
- Fear of not being able to learn new things
- Fear that you won't be able to keep up with innovation in your field

**Discover your blocks**

Here are a few questions to help you get clear on your business blocks:

- What's going on for you around social media? Is it the technology that you're scared of, or does it have more to do with being visible online in a more significant way?
- Is there a course you could take to learn how to use social media for your business effectively?
- How do you feel about learning how to use social media?
- Do you believe you're hopeless at technology? (If it's an issue of fear of being more visible online, refer to the chapter on Visibility Blocks, which will help you dig even deeper into this area.)
- What happens during workshops and training that make it difficult for you to learn new information?
- Did you experience something similar when you were in school as a child?
- Did you ever have a traumatic experience where a teacher said you were stupid?
- Did you ever have the feeling as a child that adults believed you weren't good at school or learning?
- Do you now feel too old to learn new things?
- What's stopping you from retaining what you learn in workshops?
- Are you scared of implementing new ideas in your business, or trying new things with clients?
- Did you struggle with demonstrating what you

learned in school as a child when you took exams?
- Did you have any traumatic experiences in school where you were unable to answer a question the teacher asked?
- What is it that stops you from being pleased with the success of other entrepreneurs?
- Do you honestly believe you can never achieve the level of success that they have?
- Are you afraid that other business owners in your field will take all the clients, and there won't be any left for you?
- What prevents you from seeing them as a model for success and learning from them?
- What's stopping you from hiring a business mentor?
- Are you afraid they'll tell you to do things you won't want to do in your business?
- Do you worry that their advice won't be aligned with your vision for your business?
- Do you think you'll be forced to do things that feel icky?

**Examples of blocks**

Sometimes it can be hard to identify our blocks, especially if we're just getting started digging them up. Here are some examples that might help you to identify your business blocks in the area of Learning:

- It seems like everyone else knows what to do online, but it's just so hard for me. I'll never get it right.
- Technology is hard for me. I consider myself

technophobic because I can never figure anything out. I can barely use my computer!
- I'm so tired of having to learn new things. I wish I could just run my business with what I already know.

# 18

# LIFESTYLE BLOCKS

"Go confidently in the direction of your dreams! Live the life you've imagined."

— Henry David Thoreau

When I've worked with clients in the past, I've helped them to ensure that their big business vision fits into their ideal lifestyle. There's no sense in having a successful business if you run yourself into exhaustion, making it happen. I've seen that happen to friends: they create a fantastic company that helps so many people, but they burn out in the process.

This scenario was me with my first company: we were a wildly successful, multiple seven-figure, multinational company. The media loved us—travel and spa magazines from all over the world mentioned us. From the outside, it probably looked like I was living a beautiful life. But in reality, I was working incredibly long days (during one period, from eight in the morning until after midnight), six days a week, without even one full day off in the week. And we hadn't yet started taking an actual salary from the business, so we would grab some money here and there when we could for personal use.

When we *could*—did you catch that? I had employees that had excellent salaries, and yet there I was going to the office every day with ripped tights underneath my skirt. My lifestyle hardly matched the impression we were giving off of successful business owners, and it certainly wasn't aligned with the lifestyle that I wanted for myself. It was stressful and depressing—and unfulfilling.

When I started to build my coaching business, which is what eventually evolved into what I'm doing today, I was hyper-aware of not wanting to end up burned out and exhausted, as I did with my first company. And so I went the opposite direction and was exceedingly cautious with how I spent my time as I built my business. There were many things I probably didn't do because I was subconsciously worried about burning out. I had a block around business–life balance.

Some of my clients have come to me because they're playing small with their business and lifestyle goals. They may believe they don't deserve a wildly exciting lifestyle, or they may think it's just not possible for them. This is what I mean when I refer to lifestyle blocks: anything that gets in the way of you creating the lifestyle of your dreams, whatever that means to you.

That's why I created a free resource on my website called How to Get Clear on Your Big Business Vision (you may remember it from chapter 6). It helps you to get clear on the details of what your big business vision looks like and how that fits into your ideal lifestyle. This next bit is important. You can find that among the resources for this book: http://hollyworton.com/bbb2.

### Symptoms of blocks

Here's a more detailed explanation of symptoms that you may be struggling with blocks in the area of Lifestyle. Be sure to make a note of which ones you're currently experiencing in your business.

Do any of these resonate with you?

- Your business has grown beyond your expectations. You've got a team of people working with you, but you're still struggling to get everything done each week. Between client sessions, live calls for your online program, and the admin work that "only you can do," there isn't enough time in each week. You're working long days and even weekends, and you're exhausted.
- You look at the exciting lifestyles that other online entrepreneurs live, and you know you'll never achieve that. It's frustrating, but it's just your reality.
- You started this business because you wanted a location independent lifestyle, but you can't manage to let go of all the clients who want to see you for face-to-face sessions.
- Your business is successful, and you've got a steady stream of clients. However, you still haven't managed to upgrade many aspects of your life: you've still got the same old furniture you had when you were in university, and your underwear is in a sorry state.
- You've got a wildly successful business that brings in lots of money, but you're still single—

and you don't want to be. Will you ever find the partner of your dreams?

### Common fears

Here are some common fears relating to lifestyle:

- Fear that you can't have it all
- Fear that you need to work so hard you'll never have time to relax
- Fear that family will leave you because you're working too hard
- Fear that you'll never be able to slow down
- Fear of never having the life you want

### Discover your blocks

Here are a few questions to help you get clear on your business blocks:

- Is your team working effectively and efficiently?
- Perhaps you need to restructure things?
- Are you afraid of letting go of more aspects of your business to your staff?
- What's stopping you from taking a look at that admin that "only you can do" and see if someone else can take it over?
- What's the worst that would happen if you stopped working evenings and weekends?
- What makes you think that you can't achieve the exciting lifestyle you dream of?
- What do other online entrepreneurs have that you don't?
- What are they like that you're not like?

- Are they doing something that you aren't doing?
- Is it possible that you believe you don't deserve that kind of lifestyle?
- What's stopping you from only taking on clients for Zoom, Skype, or telephone sessions?
- Are you afraid you'll lose them all?
- Do you worry that no one will want to see you for Skype sessions?
- Have you ever even tried telling potential clients that you only do remote sessions?
- What's the worst that could happen if you just drew the line and began offering only remote sessions?
- What's going on with the lack of upgrades in your lifestyle?
- Have you been investing all your business profits, or have you been spending the money on other things?
- What would it feel like to make a list of the top three things you'd really like to upgrade in your life and then actually make it happen?
- Do you have any beliefs about it being impossible to have a successful business and the perfect partner?
- Do you believe you can only have one or the other?
- What's stopping you from going out there and meeting the right person for you?
- What's keeping you from at least going out to places where you might meet someone?

## Examples of blocks

Sometimes it can be hard to identify our blocks, especially if we're just getting started digging them up. Here are some examples that might help you to identify your business blocks in the area of Lifestyle:

- Business/life balance is impossible. You can't have a successful business and also a happy and balanced family life. You've got to choose to focus on one or the other.
- It's okay to dream about lavish lifestyles and put pictures of luxury items on my vision board, but those things will never happen to me.
- It's impossible to have a successful business and a happy family and still have time for myself.

## 19

# MARKETING AND SALES BLOCKS

"The aim of marketing is to know and understand the customer so well the product or service fits him and sells itself."

— Peter Drucker

This area is a big one for many of my clients. Marketing and sales can bring up so many limiting beliefs. Clients may be afraid of really putting their energy into marketing because it will put them out there in a big way (thus triggering fears of Visibility...if this is the case for you, see chapter 24, which talks about that). And they may fear sales because they're terrified of being seen as pushy and annoying.

We can do marketing and sales can in an icky way, or we can do them in a beautiful and heart-centered way. And when it's the latter, they can have the magical effect of connecting someone in need with the perfect solution to their troubles. And that's when marketing and sales have served their purpose and done their job well.

This block was a big one for me. Because of my role within my first company, I had loads of online marketing and sales experience. But it was easy for me because I was marketing and selling something that I believed in: a gorgeous, rustic eco-hotel on the Caribbean coast of Mexico. For the right market, a stay in our hotels was an easy yes. The photos alone sold people into booking a stay with us.

But when I went into business as a solopreneur, it was all about me selling my services, and that's where the problems started. I knew the useful bits about how to market and sell my services, but it was just so damn hard. I didn't have the self-worth, self-esteem, and self-value that I needed to put myself out there and market my business, and this made things incredibly difficult. I knew what to do, but I was blocked. I imagine this is even harder for solopreneurs who don't have the years of business and marketing experience that I had when I started as a coach.

I also had many blocks around taking up *space* online—showing up too much in people's social media timelines. On a practical level, I knew this was ridiculous, because there's so much content out there these days, and people have so many connections, that we end up seeing very little of what people put out there. And yet, I cringed at being *too* visible. I didn't want people to think I was trying too hard or being too annoying. That was a visibility block that affected my marketing. As you can see, our blocks often overlap in different areas of business.

Sales can be tough, especially as a solopreneur. You're essentially selling *yourself*. Of course, you're selling your products and services, not your actual self, but it's so much more personal. You're asking people to like you and trust you, and give you their money in exchange for the help that you offer. It should be no surprise that sales blocks are pretty standard.

**Symptoms of blocks**

Here's a more detailed explanation of symptoms that you may be struggling with blocks in the area of Marketing and Sales. Be sure to make a note of which ones you're currently experiencing in your business.

Do any of these resonate with you?

- You avoid business networking like the plague. You hate the sessions where everyone has to go around in a circle and do their elevator pitch, and you hate informal networking in groups. It's all so unnatural.
- You'd love to do events like workshops and retreats, but you know you'd never be able to get enough people to fill a group. You probably wouldn't even get enough people to cover the costs, so you don't even try.
- Speaking terrifies you, so you avoid it. What if everyone hates what you have to say? That's why you turn down speaking engagements when they come to you. You always have a good reason why you can't make the event.
- You avoid doing those discovery sessions that everyone else seems to be offering. You see them as a poorly camouflaged sales pitch, and you think it's sleazy and incongruent. You refuse to do them.
- You keep thinking you should start doing webinars, but it repeatedly ends up at the bottom of your list. Between the technology and

the public speaking aspect of it, it's just too scary.

**Common fears**

Here are some common fears relating to marketing and sales:

- Fear of public speaking
- Fear of people thinking you're pushy if you sell to them
- Fear that no one will want what you have to offer
- Fear of taking up too much space in people's social media timelines
- Fear of people unsubscribing from your newsletter

**Discover your blocks**

Here are a few questions to help you get clear on your business blocks:

- What's stopping you from attending business networking events?
- Have you tried different types of groups, or did you attend one and decide to call it quits?
- What's going on with the elevator pitch for you?
- Do you hate going around in a circle and hearing everyone's minute, or are you terrified of standing up and speaking about yourself?
- What's going on for you with the more informal, conversational networking?

- Do you struggle to talk about your business coherently?
- Are you afraid of how you come across?
- What's stopping you from really stepping up your marketing in a big way: doing joint ventures and running Facebook ads to build your community so you can run events?
- Have you tried asking your current email list if they're interested in workshops and retreats?
- Have you put this idea out there at all in any way?
- What's stopping you? Are you afraid people won't be interested?
- What is it that scares you about speaking?
- What's preventing you from joining Toastmasters or some other organization that might help you to be a good speaker?
- Why do you think you're feeling insecure about your message?
- What's the worst that could happen if you spoke to a group, and they weren't very receptive?
- Do you have any icky memories from the past when you made a big mistake in a school presentation, and everyone laughed at you?
- What's stopping you from offering discovery sessions to potential clients? They can be a good way of getting to know someone and allowing them to get to know you and see if you're a good fit.
- Do you believe that all sales conversations are sleazy?
- Do you think that it's impossible to be congruent when selling to a potential client?

- How are you afraid of coming across in a sales conversation?
- Would it feel any different if you were to view them as an invitation for people to work with you?
- Would it be different if you just saw them as a way to connect with people, with no attachment to the outcome of getting a new client?
- What's going on for you with webinars?
- Is it fear of technology and speaking, or is it something else?
- What's the worst that could happen if a webinar went wrong? And what does "going wrong" mean to you?
- What do you envision in your webinar nightmares?
- Do you believe that they're just not for you?

**Examples of blocks**

Sometimes it can be hard to identify our blocks, especially if we're just getting started digging them up. Here are some examples that might help you to identify your business blocks in the area of Marketing and Sales:

- I'm terrified of people saying no to me, so it's just easier to avoid sales conversations. Being rejected is scary and awkward.
- I'm terrible at explaining what I do, so networking meetings don't work for me.
- Marketing is so stressful that it drains my energy. I'm just not good at it.

**On the podcast**

You can find the full list of podcast episodes here: www.hollyworton.com/podcast

- 255 Jo Casey + Holly ~ How to Navigate the New Era of Email Marketing
- 228 Holly Worton ~ How to Be Consistent in Marketing Your Business (And Why It's So Important)
- 218 Stella Orange ~ How to Experiment With New Ways of Marketing That Don't Feel Manipulative
- 212 Jo + Holly ~ How to Add More Depth to Your Marketing
- 203 Jo + Holly ~ How to Find New Ways of Marketing Business Online
- 179 Holly Worton ~ How to Balance Inner Work & Marketing Your Business
- 172 Elizabeth Goddard ~ How to Revolutionize Your Email Marketing With ConvertKit
- 124 Beth Grant ~ How to Align Your Marketing With Who You Are
- 106 Nicci Bonfanti ~ How to Serve Your Clients Through Selling
- 102 Halley Grey ~ How to Create Sales Pages That Work
- 50 How to Plan a Digital Marketing Strategy, with Julia Lera
- 38 How to Get More Clients Saying Yes, with Catherine Watkin

20

# MONEY BLOCKS

"When we do what we are meant to do, money comes to us, doors open for us, we feel useful, and the work we do feels like play to us."

— Julia Cameron

Money is a big part of the work that I do with entrepreneurs in helping them identify their business blocks and transforming their business mindset. But the real expert in money mindset is the fabulous Denise Duffield-Thomas. If you haven't heard of her, check her out. Now. There are so many money blocks out there that Denise has devoted an entire book to it, called *Get Rich Lucky Bitch*.

For *this* book that you're reading here, we'll stick to a very brief introduction of money blocks as they relate to business. There are many! In fact, in my book *Business Blocks*, this is the largest category of business belief statements.

Money is one of those things that we've heard about

since we were very, very small. As children, we might have picked up some money blocks from family, teachers, or friends. And growing up, we often continue to absorb the money blocks of others. Do your family and friends often complain about money? Then don't be surprised if this rubs off on you and leads to your subconscious, creating fears, blocks, and limiting beliefs around money.

If this is not our first business, we may have picked up money blocks from a previous company that struggled or failed. And if we've had jobs that weren't very lucrative, we might have acquired some money blocks there. These can come from all aspects of our lives!

My first company was very successful, but we were growing at such a fast rate that we always had significant cash flow problems and struggled to make ends meet. Money was a constant source of stress in my first business —remember that story about ripped tights from a couple of chapters ago? I formed so many limiting money beliefs during the ten years I spent in that company, and I've spent much time unraveling these blocks in the last decade.

Another money block that I developed was around creating a successful business on my own. I had co-founded my first company with my business partner, and while things were financially rocky, the business was thriving. Once I started my coaching business as a solopreneur, the fact that I struggled to make a living from my business created the business block that I wasn't capable of making money on my own (from being self-employed).

I also had plenty of money blocks around self-worth. Money had been such a problem in my first company, and I had allowed my business partner to make so many decisions that were not aligned with my values, that I developed the money block that I didn't deserve to make good money. I wasn't worth it.

## Symptoms of blocks

Here's a more detailed explanation of symptoms that you may be struggling with blocks in the area of Money. Be sure to make a note of which ones you're currently experiencing in your business.

Do any of these resonate with you?

- You always manage to bring in just enough to cover the bills, but no more. Saving money is impossible because you're just getting by. Barely.
- Your business is bringing in a steady stream of clients and money. Still, you have so many expenses that it all goes right out again: advertising, marketing, your support team, graphic design—you spend almost as much as you make in your business.
- You've got a string of failed companies behind you, and you're terrified that this business will go the way of the others, even though things have been looking good lately.
- You racked up much debt to start your business, and now you're afraid you'll be stuck with it if your business goes under.
- Your business is doing well, and you're bringing in lots of money, but deep down, you don't feel proud of what you're doing. It doesn't seem right.

## Common fears

Here are some common fears relating to money:

- Fear that you'll never have enough

- Fear that you'll go bankrupt
- Fear that you'll earn so much that people will ask you for loans
- Fear that you'll earn so much money that your friends will think you're a snob
- Fear that making too much money will turn you into a bad person

**Discover your blocks**

Here are a few questions to help you get clear on your business blocks:

- What's stopping you from generating more than just the bare minimum?
- Do you have any limiting beliefs around making MORE than enough money?
- What's happening with your lack of savings?
- Are you afraid that if you start to save money, you'll lose it somehow?
- Do you believe that you don't deserve to live a comfortable life with savings?
- What's going on with all the expenses?
- Do you feel like you have to spend as much as you earn?
- Is there anything you could cut back on? (What does that question bring up for you?)
- When you look in your bank account and see money in there, do you believe you have to spend every last penny, just because you have it?
- Do you think that you've got some business curse on you and that you'll never create a successful business?

- Are you not worthy of having a company that brings in money?
- Do you think you don't know how to build a thriving business?
- What's stopping you from letting go of your past companies that didn't make it?
- What's the worst that could happen if this business became wildly successful beyond your imagination?
- What's making you think so negatively about your business?
- Do you have a plan to create sufficient income to pay off your debt?
- What's stopping you from focusing on bringing in money, rather than your fear of debt?
- Do you feel like it's not right for you to make money when it's so easy for you to do what you do?
- That somehow you're not deserving of receiving lots of money for your work?
- Or do you have issues around you not worthy of making lots of money...easily?

**Examples of blocks**

Sometimes it can be hard to identify our blocks, especially if we're just getting started digging them up. Here are some examples that might help you to identify your business blocks in the area of Money:

- Spiritual people aren't rich, and it's more important for me to be a good, spiritual person than it is to have lots of money.

- As soon as I make any money, it just goes right out the door again.
- I don't deserve to have lots of money. That's for other people.

**On the podcast**

You can find the full list of podcast episodes here: www.hollyworton.com/podcast

- 278 Joanna Hennon + Holly ~ Success: It's More Than Just Money
- 248 Holly + Joanna Hennon ~ How to Make Money Manifesting Work for You
- 221 Holly Worton ~ How Your Money Mindset Relates to Your Business Mindset
- 170 Denise Duffield-Thomas ~ How Upgrading Your Money Mindset Can Transform Your Business
- 101 Ann Wilson ~ How to Make Your Money Work Hard For You
- 90 How to Overcome Your Money Blocks, with Denise Duffield-Thomas
- 66 How to Heal Your Money Blocks, with Yiye Zhang
- 29 How to Heal Your Money "Stuff" & Find Your Life Purpose, with Mary Jane Allen
- 18 How to Make More Money in Your Business, with Roxy Ahmed

## 21

# PERSONAL POWER BLOCKS

"Personal power ... is made up of the layers of self-trust, self-love, self-acceptance, self-esteem, self-confidence, self-value, self-worth."

— The Grandmothers, If Trees Could Talk

First of all, what is personal power? There are many definitions of it. In a business (corporate) sense, it can be the influence and authority a person has over their followers. It can also be defined as a person's strength, confidence, and self-confidence.

Joanna DeVoe defines personal power as: "allowing Source to flow through you and harnessing that energy in a way that creates positive momentum in your own life and the lives of those people you are here to serve." Now, whether or not you believe in Source/Spirit/God/the Universe/whatever you might call it, I think this is a fantastic definition.

I think we can all agree that energy exists. Then personal power would be allowing this energy to create positive momentum in our lives and in the lives of the people we are here to serve. This momentum could be both in our business and in other areas of our lives. To me, it's about our ability and our effort to make a positive difference in the world.

There's a belief statement that you learn in the PSYCH-K® Basic Workshop that goes like this: "I have the ability and responsibility to make a positive difference in the world." Now, I've balanced for this before, but the first time it came up for me it sounded so big and scary. Do I have the ability to make a positive difference in the world? Am I ready to accept the responsibility to make a positive difference in the world? I'm pretty sure I had to balance more than one belief statement around this concept before I was able to put it into action in my life.

Personal power is such a big issue for so many people, that there's an entire chapter devoted to it in my 2019 book *If Trees Could Talk: Life Lessons from the Wisdom of the Woods*. It contains a declaration to help the reader choose personal power—for good. Many people get hung up on power being negative or harmful when it's merely energy that can we can use to help or to hurt. You choose.

In the book, this message was shared: "*Personal power is a* feeling ... *and it is multi-layered. It is not something that most people will achieve overnight or after one simple visualization. It is made up of the layers of self-trust, self-love, self-acceptance, self-esteem, self-confidence, self-value, self-worth.*" I love this definition: personal power is multi-layered, and the more that we work on our mindset, the more we will boost our sense of personal power.

As you might imagine, my relationship with my first business partner left me feeling very powerless. I felt powerless to defend myself, powerless to express my values and opinions, and powerless to take the actions I wanted to take. It required years of therapy and mindset work to get me back on track, to the point where I could even begin to entertain the concept of personal power, much less feel it within myself.

In my coaching business, this showed up as me being afraid to express my opinions and my authentic voice. Yes, I was blogging and podcasting, but I was trying to keep it neutral. I avoided controversial topics that were related to my field. I had great ideas, but unfortunately, the way that I presented them was incredibly beige.

This situation is a massive symptom of someone not being in their personal power: beigeness. You know you're beige when you're not expressing your quirkiness, your sense of humor, or your true beliefs. You know you're blending into the crowd when your message is unremarkable, and no one connects with it. This was me for a long time.

### Symptoms of blocks

Here's a more detailed explanation of symptoms that you may be struggling with blocks in the area of Personal Power. Be sure to make a note of which ones you're currently experiencing in your business.

Do any of these resonate with you?

- You feel awkward when people talk about "life purpose" and "making a difference" in the world. You're just an ordinary person; what difference can you make? You want to run your own business.
- You feel small in the world of online business. There are many prominent personalities out there, and you're just little ole you.

- You've got a big vision for your business, but sometimes you feel powerless to achieve it. You're not sure you have what it takes.
- You are easily influenced by everything that you read online by all the latest business gurus. One week it's one thing, and the next week it's something else. You're being swept back and forth by the tide of all these external opinions of what you need to be doing to make your business successful. So much noise, and it's all conflicting.
- You feel anything but powerful as an entrepreneur. Plus, powerful feels like a dirty word. Only bad people are powerful.

### Common fears

Here are some common fears relating to personal power:

- Fear of being seen as a tyrant
- Fear of being attacked for your beliefs
- Fear that people won't like you if you stand up for what you believe in
- Fear that being a strong person will be a turnoff to people
- Fear of being different

### Discover your blocks

Here are a few questions to help you get clear on your business blocks:

- Why don't you believe you can make a difference in the world?

- Do you think that you make a difference in your clients' lives?
- What's stopping you from stepping up into a role where you can help people on a much bigger scale?
- What's stopping you from accepting your part in making the world a better place just as you are today?
- What's the worst that could happen if you tried to make a positive difference in the world?
- What makes you think you can't grow to the size of those prominent online business personalities?
- What's stopping you from growing into that role?
- What's holding you back from just being yourself and shining your light even brighter?
- Are you afraid of being more visible in the world?
- What gives you the idea that you don't have what it takes to achieve your big business vision?
- Who do you think you need to be to achieve this vision?
- What's stopping you from achieving this vision?
- What makes you feel powerless to achieve your goals?
- What makes it hard to focus on your business, rather than being swayed by all that you read online?
- What's stopping you from cutting out the noise and just focusing on your business and what you know you want to do?
- Do you believe you're not strong enough to

stand your ground and build your business based on your wants and interests?

- What is it about the word "powerful" that sounds dirty?
- And why do you think only bad people are powerful?
- Can you think of any examples of influential people who did excellent work in the world, and who made a positive difference?
- What do you think is stopping you from feeling powerful?
- What do you need to believe about yourself to feel powerful in a good way?

**Examples of blocks**

Sometimes it can be hard to identify our blocks, especially if we're just getting started digging them up. Here are some examples that might help you to identify your business blocks in the area of Personal Power:

- It's impossible to be both powerful and heart-centered, and I'd rather be heart-centered.
- Power isn't feminine. Only men are powerful, and I don't want to have to pretend to be a man.
- It's hard to stand up for myself when people criticize me. I don't know how to defend myself.

**On the podcast**

You can find the full list of podcast episodes here: www.hollyworton.com/podcast

- 297 Holly Worton ~ Personal Power: Why You Need It & How to Get It
- 158 Joanna Hennon ~ Get Better Results in Business by Accessing Your Soul Power
- 120 Amber Lilyestrom ~ How to Step Into Your Power Through Your Brand
- 41 How to Step Into Your Personal Power in Business, with Jac McNeil
- 9 How to Achieve Holistic Self-Empowerment, with Sofia Barao

# 22

# STRATEGY, CLARITY AND VISION BLOCKS

"At the end of the day, when it comes time to make that decision ... all you have to guide you are your values, and your vision, and the life experiences that make you who you are."

— Michelle Obama

This area is a bit tricky, and it's worth mentioning that having a clear strategy and vision for your business might involve two parts: hiring the right coach/mentor for you *and* uncovering and releasing any blocks you might have in this area. A coach or mentor can be vital in helping you craft a clear strategy for you to achieve your business vision, but sometimes we can be so blocked that we struggle to even come up with a vision for our business.

Other times, we play small, and our business vision reflects that. Again, a coach or mentor can help you to dream bigger and create a bigger vision, but if your subconscious mindset is blocked by limiting beliefs, it can make dreaming big even more difficult. Releasing any blocks you have around strategy, clarity, and vision can make the work that you do with a coach or mentor easier and even more powerful.

If you've ever invested big money in a coach, mentor, or mastermind and you didn't get great results (despite these being great professionals or programs), maybe your subconscious mindset was holding you back. If this is the case, you can do the work to transform your subconscious mindset *now* and then go back and review your notes or materials from the program or course. Doing this will help you take advantage of all that you learned and more easily implement the knowledge with your upgraded business mindset.

I've spent lots of money on business coaches and mentors that never felt quite right for me, but I was so desperate for my business to work, and they were so great at selling their services that I eagerly signed up to work with them. But because my mindset wasn't in the right place, I didn't get much out of the work, which left me feeling like a failure: I was so terrible that I couldn't even build my business with the help of an expensive coach or mentor!

This is a symptom of several issues. I felt so desperate to get help with my business that I signed up for something I knew deep down wasn't right for me, and I felt so frustrated with my situation that I allowed myself to be swayed by manipulative sales techniques. Finally, I hadn't done the mindset work that needed to be in a place to get the most out of any coach or mentor.

It's hard to get results from any coaching or mentoring program when your subconscious mindset is riddled with limiting beliefs. And even when coaches or mentors include some mindset work within their program, it's often not at the subconscious level. That's why it's so important to work with the subconscious mindset: it merely makes it easier for you to take action in your business, and when you're working with a coach or mentor, they'll usually create an action plan as a result of each session with them. If you struggle to take the actions you've agreed on, then it just makes the whole process so much more difficult and painful.

If you didn't do the exercise in Chapter 7 (How to Get Clear on What You Want), which helps you get clear on what you wanted, then now is the time to do so. You need to know what you want in your business and life because if you don't, you'll just be wandering around doing random things and getting nowhere. I think we've all been at a point in our lives when we've felt lost. That was me after I left my first company.

As I mentioned in Chapter 3, I took an extended sabbatical at this point in my life. I had a decade of business and marketing knowledge, and I knew all kinds of things about running all aspects of a boutique hotel, but I had no idea where to go from there. I didn't know what I was good at. I knew what I *could* do, but I didn't know what I *wanted* to do. I had gotten so far off track with my life that I didn't know how to get back into gear. I had significant strategy, clarity, and vision blocks.

It took over a year of trial and error and eventually moving to another country and training as a coach to finally figure out what I wanted to do (or so I thought at the time). From there, it took several years of trial and error, and pivoting and adjusting my path. Then, in 2018, I finally realized that what I wanted to do was to focus on my writing and help people with my books.

I had many blocks along the way, but I couldn't have

done it without a clear strategy and vision at each step of the way—even though my vision was regularly changing. I had to start somewhere, and then adjust my path as I walked it.

## Symptoms of blocks

Here's a more detailed explanation of symptoms that you may be struggling with blocks in the area of Strategy, Clarity and Vision. Be sure to make a note of which ones you're currently experiencing in your business.

Do any of these resonate with you?

- You're feeling muddled. You thought you were heading in one direction with your business, but it no longer feels right. You're stuck, and you have no clue which path to take forward in your business.
- You know you want to be self-employed, but you aren't quite sure what it is that you want to do. Products? Services? You know you're good at something, but what? You're ready to create a strategy to leave your job eventually, but what will you leave it to do?
- Your business feels more like a hobby than an actual company. You've got a small but steady stream of clients who like what you do, but you can't imagine how to grow this into something that would replace your part-time job, which makes up for what you're *not* earning in your business.
- You've got clients, and you love what you do, but you don't have a business model. You're just doing stuff and putting it out there in a

haphazard way, which is kind of stressful. You know that if you could just put a strategy together, things would be much easier.
- All of your clients are local, and come to see you in your therapy room. You'd love to have a more online business and see clients all over the world on Skype, but you have no idea how to make that happen.

**Common fears**

Here are some common fears relating to strategy, clarity, and vision:

- Fear of picking the wrong strategy
- Fear that you'll never be able to see a clear path forward in your business
- Fear of picking the wrong business model
- Fear that you'll never know what to do
- Fear of focusing on the wrong income streams

**Discover your blocks**

Here are a few questions to help you get clear on your business blocks:

- What's keeping you stuck?
- What is it about your previous business plans that no longer feel right?
- What would feel right for your business?
- Do you have any beliefs around not being able to choose a clear path for your business?
- Are there any beliefs around trusting your

decisions? (Also, have you worked with a business coach or mentor lately?
- The right coach/mentor could help you out of this situation once you've cleared up any limiting beliefs or blocks around strategy, clarity, and vision. This concept applies to the other points here, too.)
- What's stopping you from choosing something and trying it out?
- Do you have any fears around failure if it doesn't work out?
- Are there any beliefs about being good enough at something to charge for it?
- Are you afraid that you don't know how to create a clear vision for a business?
- What's stopping you from upgrading your activities from hobby to business?
- What's holding you back from taking this out into the world in a more significant way?
- What would your dream business look like?
- What's stopping you from dreaming bigger?
- Are there any fears around giving up a steady paycheck?
- Why do you think you struggle to create a clear vision that would transform your hobby into a business?
- What do you need to believe about yourself to turn this hobby into a business?
- What do you think is going on behind this trial and error approach to your company?
- What's stopping you from selecting a clear business model and trying it out?
- What's preventing you from hiring a coach or mentor to help you with this?

- Do you have any doubts about your ability to apply a clear strategy to your business?
- What do you think is stopping you from taking your business global?
- Do you have any fears around opening up and sharing your business with the world?
- Are there any fears around your ability to attract a wider audience?
- Do you struggle to dream bigger with your business?
- Does anything about having an online business scare you?

**Examples of blocks**

Sometimes it can be hard to identify our blocks, especially if we're just getting started digging them up. Here are some examples that might help you to identify your business blocks in the area of Strategy, Clarity and Vision:

- My vision for my business is so big that I don't believe I can achieve it.
- I know what I want to do with my business, but I can't see how to get there.
- I'm such a mess; I don't know where to go from here. It's all so confusing.

**On the podcast**

You can find the full list of podcast episodes here: www.hollyworton.com/podcast

- 195 Holly Worton ~ How to Stay Grounded + Strong in Your Vision
- 111 Holly Worton ~ How to Get Clear on Your Big Business Vision
- 50 How to Plan a Digital Marketing Strategy, with Julia Lera

## 23

# SUCCESS AND OPPORTUNITY BLOCKS

"Success is peace of mind which is a direct result of self-satisfaction in knowing you did your best to become the best you are capable of becoming."

— John Wooden

In the same way that many people fear business failure, many people also fear business success. I've seen it with so many entrepreneurs: on one level, they want to grow their business and make it prosperous; on the other hand, they fear what will happen if they do manage to create a successful business. What will their friends think? How will their families react? It's life-changing, and that can be scary.

This is also an area where past business "failures" may come up. When businesses don't work for one reason or another, they're a powerful learning opportunity. You may have heard the saying, "there's no failure, only feedback." That's true, but sometimes we can get too caught up in the "failure" and allow that to sabotage future business ventures.

This situation has happened to me in the past. On the one hand, I firmly believe that all of my business "failures" were just steps on the path to where I am today, and I learned so much from all of them. But for years, my subconscious was sending me messages that I was a business failure. Here's the full list of all of my solopreneur ventures:

- Ready to Bloom (its first incarnation)
- SMC2 (short for Social Media Coaching and Consulting)
- a social media business for nonprofits that didn't even get as far as having a name
- Tribal Hospitality (social media marketing for boutique hotels)
- Tribal Publishing (social media marketing for authors)
- Socially Holistic (social media marketing for holistic entrepreneurs)
- Ready to Bloom (in its second incarnation)
- My business that was simply under my name—until I quit *that* business to focus on my writing.

Can you see why my subconscious was screaming, "Failure! Failure!"? In reality, I can now see that this long string of "failed" businesses was simply the path to finding my thing. But that's because I've done lots of mindset work in the area of Success and Opportunity—and I can now see how every step my journey has taught me something useful to what I'm doing today.

Along the way, I also had many hangups around success being directly tied to my income. Eventually, I was bringing in the money I wanted, but I still wasn't feeling successful. I didn't have the lifestyle I wanted, and I wasn't doing the work that I wanted. I felt unfulfilled. That meant that I didn't feel successful. At some point, I was able to expand my definition of success, particularly as it pertained to my lifestyle goals. I was able to see that I was increasingly able to create the experiences that I wanted for my life, which led to me feeling much more fulfilled, and therefore successful.

Sometimes saying yes to opportunities is the key to creating the success that we want. But sometimes the possibilities are scary. Either we don't accept them, or we don't even see them when they're right in front of us. Years ago, I was afraid of public speaking (until I joined Toastmasters, but that's a story for another time). After I left my first company, I was invited to speak to a group of American MBA students about having a business in Latin America. I excitedly accepted the opportunity, and then regretted it as soon as I hung up the phone. I desperately tried to think of excuses to cancel, but in the end, I went through with it. It was a great experience, and they called me back when another university was visiting. Saying yes to this opportunity expanded my comfort zone, but I almost canceled it due to my blocks.

## Symptoms of blocks

Here's a more detailed explanation of symptoms that you may be struggling with blocks in the area of Success and Opportunity. Be sure to make a note of which ones you're currently experiencing in your business.

Do any of these resonate with you?

- You're feeling stuck and frustrated in your

business. You've been at this for some time, but things don't seem to be moving forward.

- A newsletter from a business friend pops into your email inbox. She's so excited because she's fully booked out and only has availability starting from three months from now. You're simultaneously happy for her and also more than a little envious.
- You're making enough money in your business to fully support yourself financially. Still, every time you read another entrepreneur's newsletter or look at their social media updates, it seems like they're doing so much better than you. You're constantly comparing yourself to other people's businesses.
- A friend just announced on social media that she spent the weekend on a luxury business retreat as one of the featured coaches for a big name business coach. Why does she have all the luck? You were once part of Big Name Coach's mentoring program, too. Why weren't you invited?
- Your coaching school just announced its annual conference, and several of the people you trained with are speaking at it. You love speaking, and the founder of your school knows it. Why weren't you asked to be a part of the event?

### Common fears

Here are some common fears relating to success and opportunity:

- Fear of failure
- Fear of success
- Fear of not seeing opportunities when they come to you
- Fear of picking the wrong opportunities
- Fear of being more successful than your peers

**Discover your blocks**

Here are a few questions to help you get clear on your business blocks:

- Why do you think you're feeling stuck and frustrated in your business?
- What's going on that you're not happy with?
- Do you ever feel like everyone else is successful in business, and you aren't?
- Do you ever feel like you're afraid of success?
- What's the worst that could happen if you were wildly successful beyond your dreams?
- What have you been doing to create success in your business, and what things have you been avoiding doing?
- Are any fears or limiting beliefs preventing you from taking action towards your goals so that you can create business success?
- How do you define business success? It's different for everyone, and if you see another entrepreneur living a spectacularly successful life, think about what's stopping you from adding some of the things she has to your list of goals and then taking action towards those goals?
- Have you stayed in touch with Big Name Coach

and her community since doing her mentoring program?

- What's stopping you from getting back in touch and letting her know you love what she's doing now, and you'd like to be involved if she feels like it's a good fit?
- Do you have any fears or blocks around approaching her? Might you be afraid of being rejected?
- How often do you keep in touch with your coaching school and its founders?
- Are they aware that you'd love to participate more? What might prevent you from staying in touch more, or reconnecting and letting them know that you're available for speaking? On a practical level, do you have a Speaking page on your website so that everyone knows you're available as a speaker?
- How does the idea of creating one make you feel? Are there any blocks there?
- Does that trigger any fears of visibility or rejection?

**Examples of blocks**

Sometimes it can be hard to identify our blocks, especially if we're just getting started digging them up. Here are some examples that might help you to identify your business blocks in the area of Success and Opportunity:

- I feel threatened by successful people because I fear I'll never achieve what they have.
- Exciting opportunities never come my way; no

one ever invites me to speak at their events or present to their groups.
- Success is scary; what if I lose all my friends because they don't like the new me? What if they think I'm a snob?

**On the podcast**

You can find the full list of podcast episodes here: www.hollyworton.com/podcast

- 278 Joanna Hennon + Holly ~ Success: It's More Than Just Money
- 206 Holly Worton ~ Why You've Got to Be 100% Committed to Your Business Success
- 187 Maggie Patterson ~ How to Build A Successful Business From Referrals
- 134 Linda Ursin ~ How to Tap Into Your Female Strengths For Business Success
- 107 Annie Stoker ~ How to Have Stress Free Success in Business & Life
- 33 How to Tap Into Your Success, with Linda Anderson
- 27 How to Build a Successful Business Around Your Blog, with Celestine Chua
- 24 How to Use Your Dreams for Business Success, with Tia Johnson
- 20 How to Build a Successful Coaching Practice, with Sonia Gill

## 24

# VALUE AND SELF-WORTH BLOCKS

"Over the years, I've interviewed thousands of people, most of them women, and I would say that the root of every dysfunction I've ever encountered, every problem, has been some sense of a lacking of self-value or of self-worth."

— Oprah Winfrey

Feelings of low self-worth and low value come up a lot in my sessions with clients. So many women don't feel worthy of having a successful business and making the money they want so they can live the lifestyle of their dreams. They don't value the skills and knowledge that they bring to their work.

Issues of self-worth may show up in our negative mind gremlins, and they often come from others. They can come from teachers that put us down, other adults or authority figures who criticized us as children, and even people in our lives today: partners, "friends," business partners who knock us down, and try to keep us small. You know who I'm talking about: the naysayers.

I could write a whole book on how to detox and declutter our lives from these types of people, but we'll keep it to a small part of this chapter. The important thing here is to identify the blocks that we've formed as a result of things we've been told over the years, so we can transform those blocks into new beliefs that serve us.

That business partner I've mentioned a couple of times used to say that "I wasn't even good enough to be a secretary," even though I was involved, at one time or another, in managing just about every part of our business. I had a hand in online marketing, sales, rooms division (the part of a hotel that deals with housekeeping, front desk, and maintenance), food and beverage (supervising the kitchens, restaurant, and bars), and reviewing legal documents with our legal department. I was probably involved in more than this, but these are the main areas I worked in at one time or another.

And you know what? I'm crap at many admin tasks. My brain doesn't function well with that kind of work. And my attention to detail is not great. So when he asked me to help with "secretarial" type tasks, I wasn't good at them. Why? Because I'm "not even good enough to be a secretary," following his kind of logic. Well, you can imagine the fun my subconscious had with this, creating all sorts of blocks and limiting beliefs to keep me safe in business so that I never had to deal with hearing such a comment ever again.

Has anyone in your personal or business life ever told you that you weren't good at something or that you weren't smart enough to do something? If so, the chances are that your subconscious formed a series of beliefs to keep you safe in your comfort zone, so you never had to hear something so hurtful ever again.

For me, it goes even deeper than this. I often say that "Not good enough" is my default shitty place that my mind goes to when things go wrong. This is one of the most significant overarching themes of my work, and it's not surprising that so many of my clients over the years came to me with this same issue. I cannot even begin to estimate the times that I've helped a client to balance the belief, "I am good enough." When I developed my Heart-centered Energy Work® technique a few years back, this concept was at the core of the heart center balance, which focuses on self-love, self-acceptance, and self-trust. Value and self-worth are also a massive part of this.

### Symptoms of blocks

Here's a more detailed explanation of symptoms that you may be struggling with blocks in the area of Value and Self-Worth. Be sure to make a note of which ones you're currently experiencing in your business.

Do any of these resonate with you?

- You've put together the framework for a new coaching program. Based on your experience with clients, you know this particular program is the best way for you to help people within a more structured format than just offering single sessions. You're ready to get out there and offer it to people, but you just haven't gotten around to doing it yet.
- You know you need to get a Testimonials page up on your new website, and you've got a list of clients who have already given you great feedback about your work, but you can't bring yourself to ask them for a testimonial.

- You're the cheapest person in your field. You price by the hour, and you know you charge less than everyone else who does what you do. After all, you've done the research.
- You're running your online program live for the second time this year. Everyone was happy with it when you ran it for the first time last year, but you feel compelled to add a few significant bonuses to it. After all, you're known for over-delivering.
- You've got years of experience in your field. Yet you still struggle to believe that people will pay you for what you do, and you regularly give your services for free or suggest service swaps with people you meet at networking.

### Common fears

Here are some common fears relating to value and self-worth:

- Fear of not being good enough
- Fear of not being worthy of success
- Fear of not knowing enough
- Fear of not being smart enough
- Fear that you're not ready

### Discover your blocks

Here are a few questions to help you get clear on your business blocks:

- What's holding you back from offering your new

coaching program to the people in your community?

- Do you feel that it's not good enough? Too expensive? Do you worry that no one would sign up for it?
- Do you believe that your clients don't want a big package?
- What's the worst that could happen if you picked your five favorite clients and offered them this new package?
- What's going on with your testimonials?
- Are you afraid that people might give you negative feedback rather than glowing praise?
- Are you worried that you'll bother people if you ask them for help? That they won't want to make it known that they've worked with you?
- What's stopping you from asking for testimonials?
- Does putting up praise on your website feel snobbish? (Think: "Look at me! I'm so good.")
- Why do you think it's essential for you to compare your rates to those of other people in your field?
- What do you think is keeping you at the low end of the pricing spectrum?
- Are you staying cheap on purpose?
- Do you feel like you aren't good enough to charge more?
- That you aren't worth more?
- What's the worst that could happen if you raised your rates?
- What's making you overwhelm your clients with such a robust offering?

- Are you aware that you might be suffering from Kitchen Sink Syndrome, where you throw in everything but the kitchen sink in an attempt to make sure that your clients get more than they expected?
- Does this mean that you value your core offerings so little that you have to add more, more, more?
- How do you feel about the value of your basic online program? Is it enough? If not, why?
- What's holding you back from actually offering paid services to people?
- If someone from networking (or elsewhere) has expressed interest in what you do, how does it feel to imagine quoting your prices to them?
- What beliefs do you have around receiving money for your expertise?
- Do you think you're worth it?

**Examples of blocks**

Sometimes it can be hard to identify our blocks, especially if we're just getting started digging them up. Here are some examples that might help you to identify your business blocks in the area of Value and Self-Worth:

- I'm not good enough. Everyone else is better than me at what I do.
- I don't deserve to have a successful business.
- I don't know enough yet to start charging for my services.

**On the podcast**

You can find the full list of podcast episodes here: www.hollyworton.com/podcast

- 77 How to Charge What You're Worth & Get It, with Siobhan McAuley

25

# VISIBILITY BLOCKS

"Cultivate visibility because attention is currency."

— Chris Brogan

This issue is a *huge* one with many of my clients, which is not a surprise, considering that visibility has been a big issue for me to overcome. Visibility blocks can show up in so many ways: fears of online trolls and "haters," impostor syndrome (fear of being found out to be a fraud), fears of criticism. So many things can come up when we stretch outside of our comfort zone and put ourselves out there in a more significant way because we open ourselves up to a much wider audience...and that bigger audience isn't always kind.

When you're marketing your business, whether it's online or offline, you need to be visible. Otherwise, you end up being the best-kept secret in your field. Increasing your visibility means being willing to be seen and being willing to take up space, two elements that my fabulous business coach/mentor Lisa Wechtenhiser introduced me to via work that she's done with Fabeku Fatunmise.

As I mentioned earlier, the rebranding I did in early 2016 triggered a lot of stuff for me, and it was only made possible as a result of all the mindset upgrading I've done. But still: my face was all over my website, as was my name. My face was on my Facebook cover photo and my new podcast artwork. It was everywhere. It scared the crap out of me. I was making myself super visible. I was more willing to be seen than ever before, but it was still a stretch outside of my comfort zone.

Being willing to take up space could mean physically (standing up on a stage and speaking) or virtually (showing up in people's Facebook timelines and YouTube subscriptions and inbox emails). This is *the* big issue for me: for years, I promised email subscribers that I'd never email them more than once a month because I didn't want to take up space in their inbox. I didn't post too much on Facebook because I didn't want to take up space on their timeline. The other day I posted two videos to YouTube and the same two videos to Facebook, and I felt sick. How dare I take up two videos' worth of space on someone's timeline?

Does any of this ring a bell for you? It's all about visibility blocks. I've done loads of work on my visibility blocks, and it's finally paying off. This stuff is still a stretch outside my comfort zone, but it's easier for me to take the actions.

My visibility was raised to new levels in 2019 when I released my book *If Trees Could Talk: Life Lessons from the Wisdom of the Woods.* For the first time, after having quietly released my previous eight books, I hired a public relations expert who specialized in authors. She got me an appearance on national television in the UK, which then triggered a series of other invitations to appear on radio shows in other countries, and requests to appear in or write articles for major newspapers. This was exciting.

It was also terrifying. My book was about a very non-traditional topic (talking to trees), and the coverage was a bit sensationalist at times. This triggered a lot of comments online that called me "mentally ill" and "crazy," and yet I did my best to ignore them. I was getting visible in a big way: this was what I wanted, and I was going to embrace the aftermath. It was worth it. Again, this was only possible because of the massive amount of mindset work I'd done over the years to boost my confidence around visibility. I spent the entire train journey to and from the television studio balancing belief statements.

## Symptoms of blocks

Here's a more detailed explanation of symptoms that you may be struggling with blocks in the area of Visibility. Be sure to make note of which ones you're currently experiencing in your business.

Do any of these resonate with you?

- You want to build your email list, and you've heard that a great way to do that would be to set up Facebook ads to drive traffic to your opt-in offers, but it freaks you out to think of your ads showing up in the news feeds of all those people you don't know.
- You'd love to build a YouTube channel for your business, but you hate how you look and sound on video. Plus, comments on YouTube videos can be horrendous. How could you deal with reading all those horrible things people might say about you?

- You're afraid of participating in Facebook groups; you'd like people to get to know what you do, but you're so scared of saying the wrong thing that you lurk in silence and read what everyone else has to say.
- You write regular blog posts, but you never promote them online. You're afraid of getting nasty comments on your posts...even though you could delete them if they were just trolls. The thought of getting negative comments on your writing makes your stomach churn.
- You'd like to start doing webinars, but you can't seem to get started. You've tried putting the slides together, and you keep getting stuck every time. You feel like you'll never manage to get your first webinar out there.

### Common fears

Here are some common fears relating to visibility:

- Fear of standing out in the crowd
- Fear of being seen
- Fear of getting too much attention
- Fear of criticism and negative comments
- Fear of expressing yourself fully

### Discover your blocks

Here are a few questions to help you get clear on your business blocks:

- What's stopping you from setting up those Facebook ads?

- What's the worst that could happen if unknown people saw them?
- Are you afraid of getting negative comments? Haters? People saying bad things about you?
- What kinds of negative things are you scared of people saying?
- What's the worst thing that someone could say about you?
- What's wrong with how you look and sound on video?
- What kind of offensive comments are you imagining?
- Are you afraid that people will dislike what you have to say in your videos?
- That they'll think what you have to say isn't valid?
- Are you scared that people will laugh at you?
- What do you need to believe about yourself to make it easier to create and publish videos on YouTube and Facebook?
- What's so scary about Facebook groups?
- What does this trigger for you?
- What's stopping you from speaking up and participating?
- What do you think people will say or think about you?
- Are you afraid of posting something inappropriate?
- What's the worst that could happen?
- What's stopping you from promoting your blog posts to a broader audience?
- Are you afraid that people will think you don't know what you're talking about? That your

message is too basic? That you're not good enough?
- What's going on with your webinars?
- Are you afraid that people will attend your online trainings and think you're a fraud? That they'll call you out on how little you know? That you'll be caught without an answer? That they'll say that you don't know enough to run a business around what you do?
- What's the worst that could happen if you ran a webinar and opened yourself up to people's feedback?

**Examples of blocks**

Sometimes it can be hard to identify our blocks, especially if we're just getting started digging them up. Here are some examples that might help you to identify your business blocks in the area of Visibility:

- It's scary to put myself out there in a bigger way.
- I hate the thought of getting online haters and trolls; I could never deal with that.
- I'm afraid of people criticizing my work.

**On the podcast**

You can find the full list of podcast episodes here: www.hollyworton.com/podcast

- 215 Holly Worton ~ Boost Your Visibility With Reviews, Testimonials, Referrals, & Shoutouts

- 213 Holly Worton ~ How to Face the Shadow Side of Visibility With Confidence
- 211 Holly Worton ~ How to Redefine Visibility & Create Deeper Connections Online
- 157 Holly Worton ~ How to Increase Your Visibility by Transforming Your Mindset
- 137 Holly Worton ~ How to Stop Hiding & Overcome Your Fear of Visibility
- 53 How to Raise Your Visibility, with Jenny Kovacs

# 26

# TRANSFORM YOUR BUSINESS BLOCKS INTO BUSINESS BLISS

"Personal transformation can and does have global effects. As we go, so goes the world, for the world is us. The revolution that will save the world is ultimately a personal one."

— Marianne Williamson

The first step is to become aware of your business blocks, and the power of doing the work to uncover them is that now you've got the clarity you need to transform them into business strengths. How? By releasing your blocks at the subconscious level.

Remember when I talked about how powerful the subconscious mind was at the beginning of this book? Well, now we need to harness the power of the subconscious mind so we can release these fears and blocks at that profound level.

You could do this by working with a practitioner or therapist or by doing the work with yourself. I recommend a combination of the two. I regularly use a process called

PSYCH-K® with myself to transform my business mindset, but I also work with another PSYCH-K® facilitator to help me uncover my blocks and get to the core of what's going on for me. And whenever I have a session with my coach/mentor Lisa Wechtenhiser, that also brings up loads of stuff for me to work on.

As I've said before, it's vital that you find the process or technique that works best for you. That's why I haven't included a specific process in this book: what works for me may or may not work for you. And besides, even if I were to teach you a process like Heart-centered Energy Work®, that would be a whole book in itself. The process that works for you could be PSYCH-K®, or it could be NLP, EFT, TAT, hypnotherapy, or something else. You might need to try a few different techniques before you find what works for you. I include PSYCH-K® as an example in many of my stories because that's what works for *me*.

I hope you've found this book to be useful. I've tried to keep it short and simple, so you can quickly and easily identify the blocks that are keeping you stuck in your business. Awareness is the first step, and releasing your fears and blocks at the subconscious is super essential if you want to upgrade your business mindset.

Think about the following: what does it cost you to avoid doing this deep mindset work? It's so easy to put off and just keep doing what you've been doing. But what will your business be like six months from now if you don't take action? If you don't get clarity on the mindset shifts that you need to make? If you don't make those changes?

It's time to let those mind gremlins out of their cage, where they're trapped in your subconscious mind.

**Take action today**

Are you wondering what you need to do now? I've broken it all down into five easy action steps. We've got to take action and put the time in. Transforming our mindset doesn't need to be difficult, but it isn't exactly magic. It does require an investment of time and action.

Here's how to get started:

1. Identify the core blocks that you need to shift in your business mindset, using the methods and questions described in this book. Get my first book, *Business Beliefs: Upgrade Your Mindset to Overcome Self-Sabotage, Achieve Your Goals, and Transform Your Business (and Life)*, and work through that book to get even more clarity.
2. Find the best technique for you to change your mindset at the subconscious level.
3. Find the best practitioner or facilitator to help you with this mindset transformation, and/or do the work yourself.
4. Do the inner work to transform your mindset.
5. Take action to reinforce your new mindset.
6. Repeat.

**1. Identify the blocks you need to shift**

Identify the fears and blocks that you need to change in your business mindset, using the methods described in this book. Spend time journaling to get clear on what you *do* want to experience, and which blocks you need to release in order to make that happen.

**2 and 3. Find the best process and practitioner**

This may involve trial and error. If something doesn't feel quite right, then don't go back again. You don't owe them anything. Listen to your gut feeling on this, and if you don't see changes reasonably soon, you might want to reevaluate whether you've found the best method (or practitioner) for you.

After hearing so many great things about PSYCH-K®, I was tremendously disappointed in the first facilitator I saw. It was a terrible session, and I never went back to see her again. I then sought out another facilitator, but she convinced me to try ThetaHealing® instead, which I did enjoy, but I still wasn't working with the process that I wanted to try. Finally, I found a facilitator I liked and had an excellent session with her. A week or so later, I trained in the PSYCH-K® Basic Workshop.

There are many processes and techniques out there, and there are many facilitators and practitioners of each one. Sometimes it can be tricky to find what's right for you. It can take trial and error. That's why I haven't included a specific process in this book: what works for me may or may not work for you.

Some of the processes and techniques you might like to try include:

- Heart-centered Energy Work®
- PSYCH-K®
- ThetaHealing®
- Emotional Freedom Techniques® (EFT or tapping)
- NLP (Neuro-Linguistic Programming)
- TAT (Tapas Acupressure Technique)
- Ask & Receive

- hypnotherapy
- ...and more

I've also experienced sound therapy sessions and light language sessions. In 2019, I graduated from a Shamanic Plant Spirit Healing Apprenticeship, which does what it says in the name: it taught me how to work with plant spirits for healing (which, of course, can also help to free ourselves from our blocks).

Change can be *rapid* when you're working at the subconscious and energetic levels, so there's no need to attend weekly sessions for months before seeing results. Stay alert, and pay attention to how your life and business are different since you started doing the mindset work. Sometimes significant changes occur, but people don't notice because things are going well, and they're no longer experiencing whatever it was that they wanted to let go of. That's why it's so useful to write things down in a journal.

**4. Do the training yourself**

I always recommend that people train in a process or technique themselves so they can do the work on their own. There is great power in being able to release your blocks whenever you want, wherever you want, however you want. I have spent the past several years working on my blocks regularly (at least once a week!), and I also see other professionals from time to time. In my experience, this is the perfect combination to approach releasing our business blocks.

If you've found a process that you particularly like, train in it and learn how to do it for yourself. This will require an initial investment, but it will save you time and money in the long run. You'll be able to make significant changes in your belief system, and you'll be reaping the results in your business. This process is what I mean when I say "do the inner work."

### 5. Take inspired action

When I work with clients, I always help them create a short action plan at the end of each session. This is important: no matter how much work we do to release our blocks and transform our mindset, we also have to take practical action. We can release as many blocks as we want, but if we don't *do the work* in our business, we won't automatically create change.

We still need to write the blog posts, do the videos, market our business online, and make the sales calls.

I always say this is like climbing a spiral staircase: the left step is the mindset work; the right step is the practical action. Left, right, left, right, and up we go as we build our business.

In the next chapter, I talk a little bit about how you can work with others if you feel drawn to do so. If not, I encourage you to read through the chapter, so you can at least have some point of comparison to other professionals that you may choose to work with. It helps to have an idea of how different people work so you can find what's best for you.

Remember: *you* know what's best for you! There's a reason I keep saying this: we can have the tendency to give our power away to others, but deep down, you're the one who knows what's best. Go with your gut feeling or with whatever your heart says. That's your higher self checking in with you to let you know which option is best.

**On the podcast**

You can find the full list of podcast episodes here: www.hollyworton.com/podcast

- 295 Sharon Lock ~ How to Make Mindset Work a Habit
- 276 Holly Worton ~ How to Create Your Own Personal Formula For Mindset Work & Healing
- 245 Holly Worton ~ How to Spring Clean Your Business + Mindset
- 230 Holly Worton ~ How to Make Mindset Work a Habit

## 27

## NEED MORE HELP?

"Whether it's your family, friends, community that you connect with, don't be afraid to reach out. That's my biggest advice that I can say for anyone going through any kind of obstacle or trials or tribulations. Don't be afraid to reach out and ask questions. Ask for help, because you never know where you'll find it."

— Vanessa Williams

Are you feeling stuck? If you've read this book, and are still feeling like you need more help engaging the power of your inner wisdom, read on. Or perhaps you've taken the five inspired action steps, and you uncovered some fears, blocks, or limiting beliefs that have gotten in the way of you honing your business intuition. If that's the case, get help.

**Is this you?**

Are you a coach, a healer, or a holistic therapist? Maybe you've got another type of business, and you're on a mission to change the world through the work that you do. You may be just starting in business, or you may be in the process of growing your existing business.

But you've hit a rough spot. You've done all the business and marketing training, but somehow things just aren't flowing for you. You're feeling stuck and frustrated.

All you want is more clients so you can help more people (and, let's face it, make a decent living from your business). You're starting to realize that being successful in business isn't just about knowing how to market and run a business. It's also about your mindset: making sure that your beliefs and your inner dialogue are aligned with your vision and goals.

**But it's not always that easy.**

Maybe you're struggling with:

- Lack of confidence, which leads to you procrastinating on getting your Most Important Tasks completed.
- Fear that people won't get what you do. They won't want it, or else they won't be willing to pay you for it.
- Issues around visibility and fear of standing out in the online crowd.
- Fear of overwhelm if you do attract all the clients you want and build a thriving business.
- Getting started with social media marketing,

speaking, videos, and webinars—the thought of any of this makes you cringe.
- Believing you have something precious to offer. I mean, you know you do, but—do you?

Have you ever experienced any of this?

If so, you're not alone. I struggled with this stuff when I started my second business, and until I found a solution to all of this, my business suffered.

Fortunately, I found an easy solution to all of this. One that's fast, effective, and painless. It transformed my business, and it changed my life.

Imagine how it would feel if:

- You only attracted great clients: people who know what they want and they value what you do.
- You felt nourished and fulfilled by your business, confident that you were making a difference in the world, client by client.
- You had a tribe of raving fans who were eager to sign up for your new product or service launches.
- You had a clear vision for your business that felt aligned with your purpose: 100% you.
- Your business felt like it was in flow, with a regular stream of clients ready to invest in what you have to offer.

**Sound good?**

This scenario is what I want for you. I want to help purpose-driven women entrepreneurs create the business of their dreams that allows them to live the lifestyle they want.

As I mentioned earlier in the book, I've stepped back from doing one-to-one sessions so I can focus on my writing. However, I do offer occasional sessions, as well as done-for-you mindset and energy work, in my Patreon community.

Head over to www.patreon.com/hollyworton and check it out. Please get in touch if you have any questions: holly@hollyworton.com.

### Podcast

As you've seen at the end of some chapters, I've got many podcast episodes on mindset. These episodes are a great way to deepen your understanding of your mindset and find new ways of transforming your business beliefs. Most podcast episodes have full transcripts available on the website, either to read directly or as a free pdf download (no email required).

### One-to-one work

If you're ready to get started with one-to-one sessions right now, I have some recommendations for you. These are five women that I trust entirely and often go to for sessions myself. They all work online via Skype/Zoom.

I highly recommend these five facilitators:

- Cara Wilde: http://carawilde.com
- Cazzie Dare: https://yearning4learning.co.uk/
- Claire Baker: http://happyhealthyempowered.com/
- Jo Trewartha: http://freeyourmindsolutions.com/

- Sharon Lock: http://sharonlock.com

### Take Action Today

1. Check out my Patreon and see if you're interested in how I can help you there.
2. Subscribe to my podcast (Into the Woods with Holly Worton) and listen to the episodes on mindset.
3. Find a process or technique that resonates with you and a facilitator to have sessions with.
4. Once you find a technique that you love, train in it so you can use it to work with yourself.
5. If you want to do a deep dive into your business beliefs, buy the *Business Blocks* workbook.

28

# TESTIMONIALS

I'm including testimonials from my clients so you can get an idea of the results you can achieve from doing work to transform your mindset at the subconscious level. Again, I rarely do one-to-one sessions, so this isn't about me trying to sell to you. It's about new possibilities. Remember, find the best method to use for *you*, and find the best person for you to work with on this. There's no one solution for everyone.

> I was so hopeful for results when I signed on with Holly, as I opened a business about 6 months prior. My financial and physical stress were through the roof, until Holly guided me to changing the appropriate belief statements. I have **no more chest pain, no more heavyweight stress** on my shoulders, and **my most recent month's collections at the office was $80,000**! **I am a magnet for money and success!** Thank you Holly! xo
>
> — Elizabeth D. Walker DMD, MSD

I have undertaken more traditional coaching before and found it useful but I wanted to really tap into a deeper way of working – particularly accessing the subconscious level. **I found the HEW process really powerful** during each session and focussing on how I felt during the session (and afterwards) helped tap me into other things. My instinct was to work with Holly because I resonate with a lot of the points she makes in her videos and podcast and she is a really warm person. It was also important to me that I felt like Holly was working through a lot of the same issues that were coming up for me. This authenticity was really important to me. I would definitely do more work with Holly in the future and would recommend working with her to others.

— Louisa Whitney

When I first found Holly, I was struggling to get my business to a place of success. I had the foundation in place, and had done all the "right" things, but somehow, it still wasn't working ... for me. I felt like I had a mindset limitation holding me back. After my initial meeting with Holly, even before our first working session, I received $16K in unexpected personal income – debts repaid, a royalty check, a bank refund ... after only two working sessions, I booked $43K in sales for my business, and I quit my job. That was a dream I had held for over two years, and had been working for. It wasn't magic, I put the work in, had a funnel, ads and sales conversations all set, but the results from working with Holly were literally overnight, and amazing. So much so, that had you told me that this would be happening ... to me ... I would never have believed you... in a million years. Working with Holly is seriously one of the best investments in my business and my life, that I have ever made. Thanks Holly.

— Julie Languille

Working with you has made a huge difference. In fact, I think it's made all the difference. Even if things don't feel comfortable I still persevere.

— Natasha Mann

I've had some really beneficial results from the session. The changing of beliefs about myself is really working. For the first time since I started working for myself I have confidence in the value of my services and the prices I'm quoting. It's an amazing process.

— Gill Hunt

Holly's assumption of unlimited potential and possibilities in her clients, gives her a laser focused ability to spot false limitations. Holly combines her skills with compassion and sensitivity which allows you to share yourself at a deep level. Her passion for Psych - K and her commitment to walk her talk makes her a leader in field. I recommend working with her in a heart beat.

— Cara Wilde

Since working with Holly and fully owning what I'm really about my business has been going through a big change. The transformation and higher consciousness work to help entrepreneurs find their natural Flow and abundance is now taking centre stage.

It's not only easier to share what I do now because I'm just being myself, but I created a successful online programme called The Flow Project, I've been interviewed for podcasts and invited to speak at events on the topic, and opportunities to collaborate on projects incorporating spirituality in business are opening up all the time! It feels like I turned a major corner and my business has become really exciting!

— Cathy Ballard

Holly, PSYCH-K and more importantly your kind, generous way of practicing it have been fundamental in my decluttering once and for all. OMG the peace I feel is amazing. What else can I say but THANK YOU.

You have really helped me to see and work on some fundamental issues that have kept me from moving forward with my business and my life. YOU are the bomb.

— Bibi F.

Despite over the years of my own journey of personal growth and working on myself there was one major thing that just wasn't shifting, and it was a constant negative effect on my life that I could never quite break free of despite having tried lots of things. The weird thing is that the issues that Holly worked with me on just sort of dissolved. These were big issues of a traumatic nature that it felt like my emotional and physical body just didn't want to let go of – but after working with Holly these things just melted away. What's amazing is how quickly I saw this profound change.

— Catherine Watkin

I feel more confident that I will be able to develop and achieve my dream business and attract my ideal clients. I also am experiencing more clarity about how to use social media and know that I will overcome any blocks or obstacles. Since the session I do not feel that sense of fear and paralysis when I start to approach the social media format or platforms. I feel and know the changes on a physical, emotional, energetic and spiritual level. This was the best thing I could have done for myself and my business.

— Jacqueline Conroy

Holly's process is absolutely phenomenal. I can hardly believe **how quickly things start to change** after we have a session – **I've seen results as soon as hours after working with her**! Somehow after we clear what needs to be cleared and call in what I desire I see opportunities that I missed before, move forward on ideas that I've been sitting on, and say yes to exactly the right things. It's like during a session with Holly **I realign my energy to match what I want to experience** – and so when we're done what I want can't help but appear in my world. **Absolutely magical**, do your future self a big favor and book in with Holly now!

— Joanna Hennon

## BUSINESS VISIBILITY

The following is an excerpt from my book *Business Visbility: Mindset Shifts to Help You Stop Playing Small, Dimming Your Light and Devaluing Your Magic*. It's available soon in ebook, paperback, audiobook, and workbook formats.

~

> "A star does not compete with other stars around it; it just shines."
>
> — Matshona Dhliwayo

First of all, what is visibility? It can be defined as the degree to which the public sees something. So, business visibility is the degree to which the public sees you and your business, or more specifically, your potential clients.

If you've been playing small, then you probably have low business visibility. That most likely means that you've been struggling to bring in a steady stream of clients, because your ideal clients may have never even heard of you.

Low visibility entrepreneurs often struggle to explain precisely and coherently what it is that they do, and fumble over their words when delivering their elevator pitch at a networking meeting. That's because they're fearful of being seen when they stand up to talk about themselves.

Being a low visibility entrepreneur can be awkward and difficult. But the reality is that most people probably don't even notice because, as you may have guessed, they don't remember ever having come across the low visibility business owner.

Contrast this with high visibility entrepreneurs, the big-name women in business. In the business coaching/mentoring world, the names Leonie Dawson, Natalie Sisson, and Denise Duffield-Thomas come to mind. You may or may not have heard of them, but if you haven't, I'm sure you can come up with a few names of highly visible entrepreneurs. Oprah, maybe?

These are the entrepreneurs that have thriving communities around their business. They have a raving tribe of fans who love what they do and look forward to their next podcast episode, blog post, or YouTube video. And I can guarantee you that they have a steady stream of clients.

Your business visibility is directly related to your income, because if no one has ever heard of you, then they won't be able to hire you. It's that simple.

Here's what low visibility can look like in your business. Some of these may apply to you; others may not. But they may trigger an understanding of how you're blocked and stuck in terms of visibility in each area of your business.

## Action and Goals

You avoid taking the steps you need to take to be seen with your business. Maybe you blog or podcast, but then you don't share those blog posts and podcast episodes online, so no one ever hears about them. You can count the number of blog readers and podcast listeners on both hands—and you can probably name all of them because they're your friends and family members. No one outside your inner circle knows who you are or what you do because you're not taking the right actions to make that happen.

This was me for so long. I was creating loads of content: blog posts, podcast episodes, and videos, and I *did* share them on social media, but I wasn't working to grow my audience, so not that many people saw the things that I spent the time to produce. I was visible to a tiny audience. And I struggled to grow that audience for a long time.

## Change and Growth

You've been stuck in the same place for weeks, months, maybe even years. You've been complaining about the same things for years: you don't have enough clients, you're not selling enough books, you're not making enough money. Your email list is the same size, your website visitors are the same as they've always been, and your podcast episodes are still getting the same downloads. Nothing's changed, and you haven't grown. Nor has your business. Your visibility has stagnated.

Ugh. I felt so stuck and frustrated for so long in my business. I tried working with coaches and business mentors, but I still didn't get the results I wanted. I wasn't getting visible. It took lots of mindset work for me to be able to take the actions I needed to take to get more visible. I did the work, and little by little, I started changing into the person I needed to be to choose the right actions.

Eventually, when I released my book *If Trees Could Talk: Life Lessons from the Wisdom of the Woods* in 2019, I hired a book launch manager and a publicist, and that's when I was able to get visible in a much bigger way. This was a huge tipping point for me that was only possible because I had done the inner work.

## Clients and Boundaries

You either have a handful of clients or none at all. And the clients you do have are all people that you're doing exchanges or session swaps with: they're other healers or service providers that want what you have to offer, but they're not willing or able to pay for it. The same goes for you. You're not visible enough to get the client load that you want for your business.

I've always been good at wrapping up a session on time, but I haven't always been good at dealing with late clients. In my book *Business Beliefs*, I told the very embarrassing story of my VIP client who showed up three hours late for a six-hour session. I was angry with myself for not enforcing my late policy, yet I made the same mistake the following day when she arrived late once again.

Eventually, I did the mindset work that it took to set very clear boundaries with clients and uphold them. I no longer worried when clients were late; I simply implemented my late policy, and that was that. I felt stronger and happier for doing so.

### Confidence and Self-Trust

You feel like a fraud. You've been faking it until you make it, but you haven't made it yet, and you're terrified that someone will find out that it's because you have no idea what you're talking about. You're an imposter, and your impostor syndrome is keeping you invisible.

Self-confidence has always been a big issue for me. I've often felt like a fraud—like I wasn't good enough to do whatever it was that I was doing. I wasn't good enough to help people with social media, I wasn't good enough to help people with business, and I wasn't good enough to write these books. The fact that I received excellent feedback on my work wasn't enough to convince me otherwise.

After doing the mindset work to boost my self-confidence and self-trust, I slowly began to feel more and more confident in myself. I was able to do my work with ease, trusting that I had the skill and knowledge to do the things I was doing in my business. Finally, the business felt good.

### Creativity

You have plenty of ideas, but you do nothing with them. You don't blog, you don't podcast, you don't create videos for your YouTube channel. You simply don't create content. Maybe you don't even have a website. Your creativity blocks are keeping you from being visible in the world.

This isn't an area that I've struggled with; I've always been a creative person. My issues with creativity aren't so much being blocked from creating things like podcast episodes or books, but rather believing that my creations are good enough to publish. I've always enjoyed creating podcast episodes, blog posts, and YouTube videos.

But doing the mindset work made it much easier for me

to create these types of content, and to release them out in the world. It especially made it easier for me to share them online, and promote my creations so people would actually find out about them, rather than quietly publishing them and then forgetting about them.

### Leadership and Outsourcing

You're busy, busy, busy, filling your days with admin. There are so many things to do when you own a business, and you're doing all of them. You've heard of such a thing as virtual assistants, but you know deep down that no one else would do things as well as you do. Your leadership and outsourcing blocks are keeping you so busy that you don't have the time to do the essential things that will get you visible.

I haven't always been a leader, but I certainly learned to be one in my first company. Yet I never saw myself as a leader until recent years. There were many situations in which I stepped up as a leader, yet I couldn't see it in myself.

After much mindset work, I was able to see myself as the leader that I already was. I was able to step up in a more significant way and shine my light out into the world. I was able to allow myself to be seen as a leader.

### Learning

There are so many things to learn when you start your first business. And there are so many things to learn even when you're an established business owner—that is, if you want to keep innovating. Many people have blocks around learning new things, especially technology. And there's plenty of technology in any kind of business these days.

I've always been a good learner, so I didn't have many blocks in this area, but I have seen plenty of clients struggle with learning in their business as a result of previous trauma in the early years of school. At some point, a teacher or authority figure had told them they weren't a good learner, and they took on that belief for themselves.

Doing work to release past trauma can be incredibly healing. We can't delete the experience from our memories, but we can remove the associated trauma. This is a straightforward technique that you can accomplish using processes like PSYCH-K® or TRE (Trauma Release Exercises).

**Lifestyle**

You quit your job to run your own business, but now it seems like you're working harder than ever. Sometimes we trade our job for an even harder one. The only difference is that now *we're* the boss, but we're working even longer hours than before.

This was a significant problem for me in my first company: I lived in paradise, but I couldn't enjoy it because I was working from 8 am to 1 am every single day. I was ridiculously stressed out, despite owning and operating a resort and spa. I was working hard so that other people could relax.

When I started my various solopreneur ventures, I went the complete opposite direction and became very careful about how I spent my time so that I could avoid burnout. It wasn't only after much mindset work that I was able to find a happy medium, where I could work intensely and get things done, and then take time off to relax.

### Marketing and Sales

You hate marketing, and you're terrible at sales. You're terrified of asking for money for your services, and you don't want to be one of those annoying and pushy salespeople. You avoid business networking like it's the plague; you hate those ridiculous elevator pitches people are expected to give.

In my first company, I was always good at sales and marketing. But when I began my first small business as a solopreneur, it was hard for me to market myself. It just all felt too personal.

After much mindset work around marketing and sales, I improved in marketing my services—and my books. For my ninth book, I was able to hire an excellent publicist, who got me on national television in the UK, which brought me so much more visibility than I had experienced before.

### Money

Business owners with low visibility often struggle to bring in a consistent amount of money each month, experiencing spurts of income and then dry spells. That's because they haven't yet made an impact on their potential clients. They may take isolated actions that bring in clients—like giving a talk—but they aren't doing it on a regular enough basis to leave a lasting impression on anybody.

I have had significant money blocks ever since my first company. Before that, I was an excellent custodian of money: I made money, I saved money, and I invested it in having great experiences, like when I studied abroad in Spain in university. But my business partner in my first company was ridiculously bad with money, and that infected me with poor money management practices that I have since struggled to unlearn.

Little by little, after much mindset work around money, I have improved. I'm bringing in more and more money from my company and my books, and I've got a much better handle on how I manage it all. I'm feeling more confident, and I'm proud of how far I've come, after a decade of poor money practices in my first company.

### Personal Power

You feel small and unimportant. You'd like to do great things in life, but you don't believe that you can. You see online influencers and online business gurus, and you know you could never be like them. You silently follow them and observe how they do things, hiding in their shadows.

I have often shied away from standing in my power and speaking my truth. I have regularly watered down my message. I have often toned down my true colors until I looked like a murky shade of beige.

Mindset work has helped me to stand out. It's helped me to say yes to television opportunities, even when I knew I'd be criticized for my beliefs. It's helped me to write these books and others, and share my unfiltered experiences with readers.

### Strategy, Clarity, and Vision

You have no idea where you're going with your business. You know what you like doing, and you want to do that thing. How are you going to make money doing it? Who knows. They say that if you do the job you love, the money will follow—won't it?

After I left my first company, I had no idea what I wanted to do with my life. I had so many skills, and I had learned so many things, but I had no idea how to apply that to my life. I was so out of touch with myself that I didn't even know what I wanted to do.

Eventually, I ended up on the coaching and personal development path, which led me to my mindset work and finally to where I am today, living life as an author-entrepreneur. At each iteration of my business, I had a clear vision and strategy, which I continued to refine along the way. I adjusted the details and pivoted on my path, and my vision became more and more refined.

**Success and Opportunities**

Opportunities occasionally come your way, but you don't always take them. They're not quite right, you know? And you certainly don't feel successful.

For *years* I felt unsuccessful. I kept working hard, and putting in the hours, and doing the mindset work, and I still wasn't seeing results. It was disheartening, and I thought I'd never make it. I kept comparing myself to others, and that only served to bring me down.

But I kept at it. I persevered, and I refined my vision and my strategy, and eventually, I started to feel things shift. Opportunities started coming to me, and I kept saying yes. And then, there was a turning point. I began to feel successful.

**Value and Self-Worth**

You *think* you're good at what you do, but so are a lot of other people. Your prices are low because you want to keep them reasonable, and many of your clients are quite honestly friends that you're doing swap sessions with. You're not good enough to charge more.

This has been one of my biggest lessons. It's been one of the most significant areas that I've been working on in terms of mindset. "I'm not good enough" is my default shitty place that I go to when I'm feeling down. It's the motto of my mind gremlins.

After much mindset work, things started to shift in this area for me. It was something that I had to keep coming back to, as I peeled the layers of lack and low worth and went deeper and deeper with my mindset work. I can't say that I'm 100% there yet, but I've experienced massive shifts in terms of how I value myself.

## ABOUT THE AUTHOR

Holly Worton is a podcaster and nine times published author. Her latest book, *If Trees Could Talk: Life Lessons from the Wisdom of the Woods*, went straight to the top of 16 Amazon bestseller lists, and she has been featured on BBC Radio Scotland and on prime time national television in the UK – on ITV's This Morning.

She helps people get to know themselves better through connecting with Nature, so they can feel happier and more fulfilled. Holly enjoys spending time outdoors, walking long-distance trails and exploring Britain's sacred sites. She's originally from California and now lives in the Surrey Hills, but has also lived in Spain, Costa Rica, Mexico, Chile, and Argentina. Holly is a member of the Druid order OBOD.

Holly ran her first business for ten years, building it up to become a multi-million-dollar enterprise. When she went into the coaching world she was confident that she had the business and marketing skills she needed to set up a new company. And she did – but she struggled to grow her new venture quickly because she encountered fears, blocks, and limiting beliefs that she didn't even know she had.

She discovered that pushing forward and taking action just wasn't enough. She needed to transform her mindset and release her blocks, as this was the only way to take the *right* actions to move her new business forward. Thus began her journey of intense personal development through deep mindset work, which transformed her existing coaching business into a focus on helping people with their business mindset.

Eventually, she realized that she wanted to devote her time to helping people through her writing, and she let go of her mindset business to focus on her books. Now, Holly continues to write about mindset, long-distance walking, and connecting to Nature.

**Podcast**

You can find her podcast on Apple Podcasts, or wherever you listen to podcasts. Links to subscribe, as well as the full list of episodes, can be found here: http://www.hollyworton.com/podcast/.

**Patreon**

You can join her online community where you can receive the benefits of her done-for-you mindset work, and also get discounts on one-to-one sessions, by joining her on Patreon: https://www.patreon.com/hollyworton.

**Books**

You can find her other books, including her books on nature, walking long-distance trails and business mindset, wherever you purchased this book.

**Newsletter**

Finally, you can stay in touch by subscribing to her newsletter on her main website: http://www.hollyworton.com/.

amazon.com/author/hollyworton
facebook.com/HollyWortonPage
twitter.com/hollyworton
instagram.com/hollyworton
goodreads.com/HollyWorton
bookbub.com/profile/holly-worton

## ALSO BY HOLLY WORTON

### Business books

*Business Beliefs: Upgrade Your Mindset to Overcome Self-Sabotage, Achieve Your Goals, and Transform Your Business (and Life)*

*Business Beliefs: A Companion Workbook*

*Business Blocks: A Companion Workbook*

### Coming soon

*Business Intuition: Tools to Help You Trust Your Own Instincts, Connect with Your Inner Compass, and Easily Make the Right Decisions*

*Business Intuition: A Companion Workbook*

*Business Visibility: Mindset Shifts to Help You Stop Playing Small, Dimming Your Light and Devaluing Your Magic*

*Business Visibility: A Companion Workbook*

### Nature books

*If Trees Could Talk: Life Lessons from the Wisdom of the Woods*

*If Trees Could Talk: Life Lessons from the Wisdom of the Woods — A Companion Workbook*

### Walking books

*Alone on the South Downs Way: One Woman's Solo Journey from Winchester to Eastbourne*

*Walking the Downs Link: Planning Guide & Reflections on Walking from St. Martha's Hill to Shoreham-by-Sea*

*Alone on the Ridgeway: One Woman's Solo Journey from Avebury to Ivinghoe Beacon*

*Walking the Wey-South Path: Planning Guide & Reflections on Walking from Guildford to Amberley*

## A REQUEST

If you enjoyed this book, please review it online. It takes just a couple of minutes to write a quick review. It would mean the world to me! Good reviews help other readers to discover new books.

Thank you, thank you, thank you.

Made in United States
North Haven, CT
27 May 2022